Foreword
A personal connectio

Hello gentle reader ar   r!
(Cornwall, I love you!
pictures, from Califor   3
in England's most bea....   h
I am not Cornish (well, only 2.5% according to my DNA
results), this beautiful land of sea and sun reminds me
of my childhood in southern California. Discovering
Cornwall and the West Country revived in me, a
spirituality that was put away for many years.

As a child, I was intimately familiar with the sun and
sea. My Roman Catholic upbringing reinforced this
connection, teaching me that my appreciation for the
planet is *intentional*. Sitting in nature created a space in
my own mind where I felt a greater force was at play.
Heading west led to a spiritual awakening that has
inspired me to continue cultivating a peace that is
spirituality rooted in nature.

Today, more than ever, we need people to be *people of
peace*. This is a book dedicated to the practice of peace.

As a mental health therapist, it is good to see that GPs
are now prescribing time in nature. What are they
actually prescribing to the dis-eased? Peace. People are
not at peace. Many suffer with illnesses that are
physically damaging, while others have mental health
issues that are just as debilitating. Both cause an
imbalance in the body and mind. This imbalance cannot
be cured solely with medication or talking therapy, I'm
afraid. As useful as they are for many, they have their

limits. *Nature therapy* is the practice of cultivating a playful, respectful and mystic view of *nature*. This planet is a living organism and there is a force, an energy, *a chi* that governs all living and non-living matter. Humans are not at peace with *it*, in fact, we are fighting against *it* constantly!

Encouraging visits to natural places and holy sites are part of the guidance I provide to individuals seeking deeper spirituality, peace and contentment.

My own journey into nature-therapy and spirituality began in 2015 when my husband took me to Cornwall. From the moment I arrived, I felt a profound connection to the land. The rugged cliffs, and crashing waves spoke directly to my soul. On our first day there, I couldn't wait and ran into the sea where I frolicked like a child for over an hour. That night, I had a deep and restful sleep. Something I hadn't had in seven years. From then on, I just wanted to be in nature. My desire to explore natural landscapes brought me a tremendous feeling of contentment and peace. I spent the following years studying transpersonal psychotherapy and working in a more holistic way. I opened my mind to Reiki, yoga, tai-chi, eclectic dance, vulva clay sculptures (bet you didn't expect that!) and much more. Today I work as a transpersonal psychotherapist and connect people with that healing force. There are times when I can feel Cornwall calling me- *a pull I cannot resist*. I love going to Cornwall so much that I now guide people around the many magical and healing landmarks the West Country has to offer, ending in Cornwall. Its

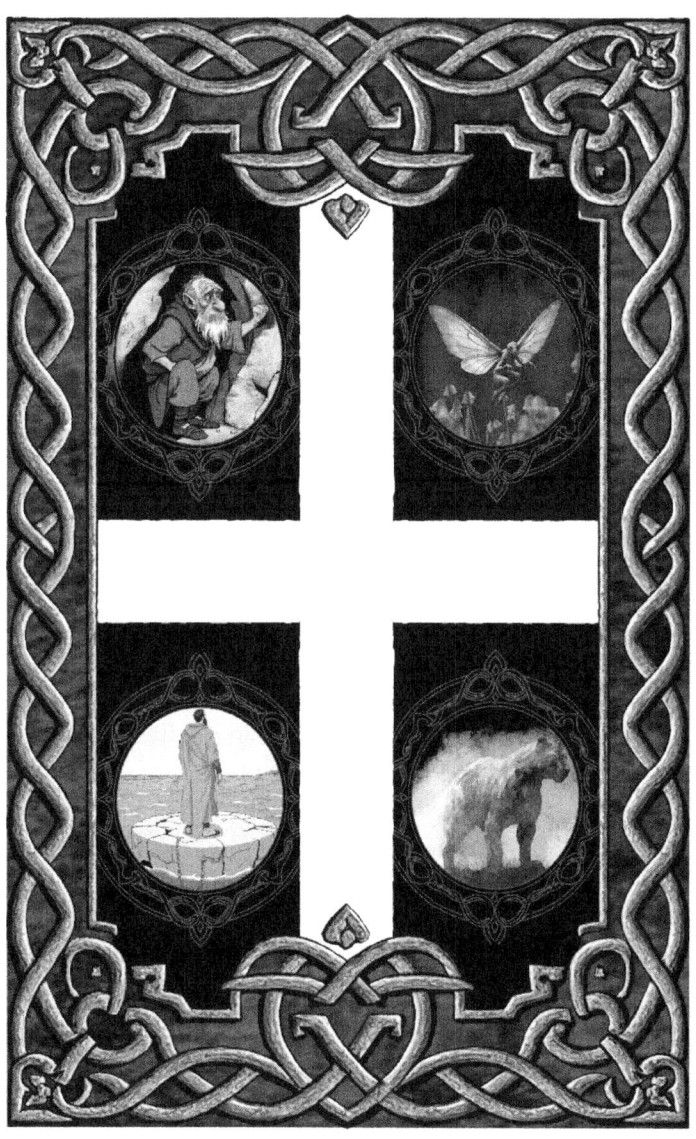

Cover by Kai Powell Copyright 2025

Kernow My'Athkar! (Cornwall, I love you!)
A Spiritual return to the West Country

by Victoria E. Karp Copyright 2025

Cover Illustrated by Kai Powell Copyright 2025

This book is dedicated to my beloved family, especially my dear husband and my cherished Aunt Patty. Your unwavering support and boundless love have been the guiding light through this incredible journey. I am forever grateful for your presence in my life, AGAPE

Thank you, Kai. Your talent as an illustrator and your knowledge of the mystic were instrumental in bringing my ideas and visions to life.

ji

The Nearly There Trees

Cornwall: Twinned with Heaven

Content

Forward: A personal connection

The Journey West

legends and folklores inspire and delight making me feel part of something bigger.

It has become a tradition to play Aretha Franklin's *Say a Little Prayer* when we reach the *Nearly There Trees* on top of the hill. I always dedicate the song to Cornwall. My senses open and I am aware the natural mystic within these parts. Cornwall has not yet been overrun by modern life. Here you cannot avoid nature, *she* is all encompassing and spectacular.

Here you will also meet many like-minded travellers who are also drawn to its beauty, mysticism, and spiritual energy.

In the following pages, I will share with you my experiences and understanding of the West Country and its deep connection to an ancient mystic. I want to inspire you to seek and develop your own natural and spiritual connection, wherever you are.

Today, as I reflect on my journey with Cornish culture and history, I believe that a patient spirit guide has been leading me back to Cornwall. This did not happen by chance. I did not come to England because of Cornwall; I discovered Cornwall as part of a deeper desire to connect with nature and heal myself.

Touching the water after a long journey
Perranporth Beach, Cornwall

I now keep a tiny tin faerie and a small tin pasty hidden safely in my wallet as a souvenir and for protection just in case…. *Just in case of what*? You may ask.

Well let me first tell you what I know of this far away land. Many people have never heard of Cornwall let alone been there; although thanks to social media and recent television series such as Poldark and Doc Martin, it has become more popular than ever before. Cornwall is located at the very westerly tip of southern England. It is considered by many Brits to be the perfect location for a summer staycation. Summer-after-summer, the beaches fill up with visitors from all over the UK and beyond. Towns and villages become overwhelmed with tourists leaving the locals to moan at the lack of amenities and space. We, the tourists, do inconvenience them terribly and the traffic at this time of year is considerable and unfortunately unavoidable. Long queues to get anywhere are commonplace. The only way to get to Cornwall from England is by train, car or flying in on a tiny plane. There is no big tourism here! Then you have to get around Cornwall and this is not easy for many reasons, so it's best you go with someone who knows it well, at least initially. Country lanes that only accommodate one vehicle at a time are commonplace, so bear this in mind if you're taking your Chelsea tractor: that's British slang for Range Rovers and cars of that size! There are plenty of trails for ramblers if you prefer to explore on foot, including the Saints Trail, but you must, and I cannot emphasize this enough, you must know where you are going to avoid any accidents or getting lost. Cornwall does not suffer fools gladly. The weather can turn on you too. Many summer holidays have been ruined by prolonged periods of rain and cloud, bringing the temperature and the mood down. Don't worry though, there is plenty to do on a rainy day as Cornwall is not just a beachy destination!

From California to Cornwall
I grew up in southern California and it is a widely accepted fact that when Californians visit Cornwall, we fall in love with it. There seems to be a strange connection between the wild western shores of the Atlantic and the wild western shores of the Pacific. It is hard to believe that Cornwall would have anything in common with California, but it has. Even as recently as the early 1980's, California was still wild and uninhabited. This is the California of my childhood.

Cornwall's landscape sometimes reminds me of it. As a child, I had a deep connection with the Pacific Ocean. There was rarely a week when I was not swimming in it or playing on the beach. I crave windy beaches because that is what California is like-especially in the winter: windswept! I knew all the caves and where to find the octopi. I would count the starfish on the rocks and collect jellyfish with a net. The beach I played on had thousands of pacific sand crabs. I used to bury my hands in the sand and scoop them up before tossing them back in the water.

The Pacific Ocean in southern California is always cold, deep and dark-unlike the green blue waters of the Cornish coast that benefit from the warmth of the jet stream. It is quite the opposite in California. The cold current comes down from Alaska, making California the ideal place for whale watching and sailing. I still remember swimming in the Children's Cove and seeing a small black head with shiny and twinkly black eyes pop out of the water next to me. It was a young seal! It stayed by my side as I swam back to the beach, disappearing once I stood up on the sandy shore. I still remember picking up those fishy notes off the seal's breath! Yes, that's how close I was to the little fellow! It was normal in those days to find yourself swimming amongst the seals.

Nowadays that beach is closed to the public as the seals and sealions have reclaimed it. Good for them! The smell is stronger than ever too. You can't miss it as you walk down the hill that takes you to the little cove. Like San Diego, Cornwall's residents don't just include humans! Seals, whales, sharks, eagles and wild hares also call this place home. Then, there are the spiritual energies that live within its interior and sandy shores. Elemental beings, nature spirits and ghosts all live here too, if, you choose to see.

Above: Seals in the Children's Pool, La Jolla, California
Below: Pacific Beach, Sand Diego, California, Circa 2004

Above: Children's Pool La Jolla, circa 1990
Below: Cliffs with wildlife below, La Jolla circa 1992

Above: Seals on a rock, La Jolla circa 2003
Below: My children on a windswept beach, Cornwall 2016

A nautical connection

The navy is another link between my childhood in America and Cornwall. My hometown of San Diego is also the home of the United States Navy Seals. Like San Diego, Cornwall has a strong naval history. Trebah Gardens, for example, was home to the US navy in preparation for the D-Day landings. This is by far one of my favourite gardens in Cornwall. The beautiful pebbly beach below hosts crystal clear waters with serene views of the bay ahead. You can have a swim or just tread the clear waters taking in the nature all around you.

View from Trebah Gardens, Cornwall, 2019

What is a pirate's favourite letter? *Arrrrrrrr!* Records show that Cornish sailors, like many of their English and Scottish brethren, were known to resort to piracy from time to time. Sir Francis Drake, the English explorer and privateer, is a hero to the British, but to the Spanish and French, he's a notorious pirate. The English were not alone in the business of piracy; the West Country's coastline has a long history of foreign attacks too, dating back to the Vikings. Since then, French, Spanish, Danish and even North African pirates have raided these shores!

Today, you are perfectly safe navigating these waters. If you want to learn more about the link between sea and song, then come along to the annual Sea Shanty Festival. It takes place yearly in Falmouth town. All along the high street, every pub and street corner will have a group of people belting out tunes in unison. Tales of passing the Cape horn, mermaids, lost loves and of course, buried treasure are what sea shantys are all about! To think I grew up listening and singing along yet never knew where they were from.

Market Square,
Alton, Hampshire 2025
I took part in an all-female
Sea-shanty choir
Conducted by author and
singer-songwriter,
Anna Tabbush.

A beauty rooted in nature.

Cornwall's beauty extends beyond the sea. Its isolation and distance from the rest of England has helped preserve an ancient wilderness now lost to the modern world. Here, I am in constant communication with it. For generations, these shores, woodlands and moors have inspired writers, painters, sculptors, nature lovers and spiritualists alike, yet few people today appreciate the mystery of this land and its people. Cornwall invites you to develop a spirituality routed in nature. Many come here on pilgrimage, following the Saint's Trail along the coast. It seems impossible to not feel connected to something magnificent. It came as no surprise to me when I found out that Cornwall has the most concentration of saints in the whole of the UK. Even today it continues to welcome those seeking guidance, spirituality, and healing.

Cornwall and the West Country

The borders that mark the West Country are loose, however it is fair to say that it begins around the Bristol Channel taking in parts of Gloucester to the north and Wiltshire to the east, while further south, Somerset turns into Dorset and both border Devon. From Devon, the West Country narrows noticeably into deepest, darkest Cornwall. As you pass the tree copse on the hill just past Launceston, you will pass an important marker that symbolizes the spirit of '*nearly there'*. So many of us smile and give thanks when we arrive.

As you have worked out, falling in love with Cornwall is easily done. But will it love you back? Some go and return disappointed, while others are truly welcome here. I fell in love with Cornwall, and I know it loves me back. If it chooses to love you, you may never escape it, and I am sure of it. We are in short supply of nature lovers and those seeking higher spirituality but in Cornwall, we can still find a quiet sanctuary. I am always happy here, even on a dark, rainy Tuesday in February!

For me, Cornwall is not just for the holidays, it is for every day. Discovering Cornwall turned out to be a spiritual discovery too. I now carry Cornwall in my heart. I could not agree more with my friend Joe when he said, *'Being in Cornwall is like pushing the reset button on myself.'* We all deserve a chance to do that. It is not just the land, the people and their spirit of community keeps this remote part of England tightly rooted in tradition and identity. For me, Cornwall helped me put into perspective what really matters: finding communities that also share my values and beliefs. A spiritual awakening is not a call you can easily ignore. How marvellous to find myself in love and in faith. I know that when my time comes to say goodbye to this body and this life, my spirit will fly over Cornwall one last time.

Faerie Stacks on Perranporth Beach, 2019

Part One

Blow, blow, westerly wind.
Take me out where the ocean rolls without end.
With the wind in my sails and the sun on my back,
Let us haul, haul, away Jacks!

Cornish Sea Shanty by Anna Tabbush

Chapter 1
West is West.

The spirit of the West Country of England is free and untameable. This land of sea and cliffs marks the great frontier between east and west. Europe ends and the Atlantic ocean takes over. It is a constant companion as you travel these lands. The spirit of nature also lives here, among its flora and fauna. But make no mistake. This Eden is *a frontier land* where men are outnumbered by animals and mystic beings manipulate the landscape.

Devon and Cornwall both had a reputation for harbouring highwaymen and privateers. The foggy moors were ideal places to wait and pounce on vulnerable travellers. Ships full of brandy, rum, tea, and spices could easily hide within the numerous secret beaches and passages known to a select few. Criminals often escaped the long arm of the law by hiding out in deepest, darkest Cornwall, taking their chances within its difficult terrain, haunted moors, and enchanted woodlands.

Travelling through this land will bring you face to face with abandoned mines and lonely headframes-symbols of an industry that once thrived here. Yes, the land has been mined like a Swiss cheese, so you must be careful where you walk. Do not go wandering off-piste as you may fall down an unmarked pit. If you do visit the empty mines, you may still hear the *knockers* if you knock on the rock and leave them a bit of food. Oh, but they are cross with us! We have abandoned them with many modern folk forgetting altogether. So, let us remember Cornwall and the Cornish whose lives changed the world. That is right, Cornwall is everywhere. From Australia to South Africa, the Cornish have passed down their language, traditions, and beliefs.

A long way from home, Jack
Our first story begins about two hundred years ago and over five thousand miles away from Cornwall. It is 1828, we are at the height of the British Empire, and yet, 20% of Cornwall's population is leaving in search of opportunity and fortune outside of Britain. Mining at home has become one of the only sources of income with heavy competition and terrible conditions. Many Cornish men and their families set sail for the United States, where they followed the gold rush all the way to Colorado, Utah and then California. The British Empire recruited others to work in mines across South America, Australia, and Africa.

One such group of Cornish miners and their families were recruited from the towns of Camborne and Redruth to work in Mexico. Renowned for their expertise in mining ore, these *Cousin Jacks* and *Cousin*

Jennys, as they were affectionately known, were welcomed and admired by the locals at the Purissima Real del Monte mine. Their legacy remains unmistakable even today. Imagine, a Cornish town nestled in the tropical mountains of Mexico? What an unexpected yet fascinating sight!

I came across this historic town while travelling as a student. My friends and I heard all about an English mining community nestled up in the mountains. We took the coach up a steep and winding road along the misty mountains known as the *Sierra de Pachuca*. After three hours we arrived at the brand new Hotel Real del Monte. It was a rainy and foggy day but it did not take anything away from the beauty of our surroundings.

A stroll along the high-street made us feel as if we had been transported to a quaint and picturesque British town. Such was the influence of those early settlers that even the local delicacy is a pasty! For those who do not know, a pasty (pronounced paz-tee) is a 'D' shaped meat pastry eaten by the Cornish working class. It got its name from the French who introduced pastry work to England and the Dutch who brought hardy root vegetables like the suede and turnip to feed Britain's hungry masses. Loved by many and considered a heartwarming comfort food, the pasty is the original fast-food! Savoury, warm and easy to eat quickly, it is the ideal food for workers on the go.

Over time, the pasty evolved to incorporate local ingredients. A Mexican pasty is filled with beans and cheese or chicken and spices. These little pies are a delightful example of the wonderful fusion of Cornish and Mexican culinary traditions.

Above: Walking down the Avenida, Real del Monte, 2002.
Below, left to right: Cornish Pasties; Church, Real de Monte, Mexico, 2002

Down the Mine

Later that afternoon, a small group of us booked tickets to visit the famous mining museum. To my surprise, the tour included a ride down the shaft to the pit, where we could see firsthand how the miners once worked. With high-visibility jackets, helmets, and torches, we followed the guide into the lift. The descent was steep—approximately 170 meters into the earth. As the lift doors opened, we found a darkness so complete it swallowed everything. It was cold, and the air felt dense and stale. Our torches illuminated the narrow tunnels as we ventured deeper, traveling four hundred meters underground. The oppressive silence and trapped air were constant reminders of how unnatural this environment was for human life.

The guide shared interesting facts about the mine's history including beliefs and folklore practiced here. He spoke of unexplained noises and knocking sounds echoing through the tunnels. Reports of strange lights appearing unexpectedly have been recorded by tourists and workers alike. We dismissed his stories as theatrics, meant to add drama to the tour. At one point, we came across a small shrine carved into the rock, a humble but reverent space. The guide explained that the miners had built it to honour the spirits of the mine, whom they called *knockers.* These spirits would alert the miners of an impending danger, such as a collapse. In exchange, the miners left offerings such as coins, pasty crusts, and small tokens to show their respect and gratitude. Although I was not prepared for this part of the tour, I rummaged through my pockets and found a few pesos and some mints wrapped in gold foil. It felt meagre compared to the offerings left by those who came before me, but I emptied my pockets and placed them at the shrine, hoping my small gesture would suffice.

Standing in the 'Rich Mine', as The Cornish called it, Real del Monte, Mexico,2002

We moved deeper into the tunnels, feeling the cold seeping into our jackets. I remember thinking how extraordinary and terrifying it must have been for the miners to spend entire days and nights in such conditions. What truly captures your attention in the mine is the silence. It is not just quiet, it is unnervingly quiet, a silence so profound it becomes deafening. It is human nature to fill that void with imagined sounds, convincing ourselves we heard something. At some point, we did. A faint knocking sound echoing through the tunnels. Our curiosity got the better of us and we decided to explore on foot. As we approached the shrine, we all saw something. It was a moving shadow but I did not find the thing that cast it. It darted across the shrine and disappeared into the rock before we could shine our torches on it. We froze, unsure if what we had seen was real or a trick of the dim light. But as we got closer to the shrine, I noticed something odd: my mints were gone! So were the coins!

Then, clear as day, we heard three sharp knocks from one of the tunnels. The sound reverberated through the still air, but no one was there. Before we could even react, a cold breeze swept past us. It was not just cold, it was unnatural, chilling us to the bone. How could there be a breeze when we were deep underground, in an abandoned mine, where no air should flow?

We walked along this long corridor which runs for miles.
Real del Monte, Mexico, 2002

My nose started to run from the cold, and my hands and feet felt numb. As I searched my pockets for a tissue, an overwhelming sense of dread took hold of me. It felt as though something was watching, following and closing in. The others felt it too. Without a word, we all knew it was time to leave. We tried to stay calm, but the unspoken fear drove us to a hurried, clumsy pace as we made our way back to the train. My heart pounded in my chest as I felt the weight of the dark pressing against my back. When we finally reached the train, I collapsed into my seat and shut my eyes, desperate to escape the oppressive feeling. But even then, I heard it again! A knocking on the rock above me. The sound sent a shiver down my spine. I squeezed my friend's hand, as she squeezed back, her fear mirroring mine. Relief washed over us as we stepped into the lift and began our ascent back to daylight. When the first rays of sunlight touched my face, I inhaled deeply, savouring the crisp, fresh air. The panic that had gripped me moments before melted away, leaving me to wonder if it had all been in my head. Maybe it was just a bout of claustrophobia. After all, isn't it normal to feel uneasy when you are trapped hundreds of metres underground?

We laughed nervously, brushing it off as a clever trick orchestrated by the guide to make the tour more memorable. But the guide vehemently denied it, swearing he had no part in what we had experienced. He spoke of the spirits that have dwelled in the mines for centuries, long before the miners arrived. The Cornish, who were used to nature spirits, knew how to deal with them. The shrine was there to honour and give thanks to *the knockers* for looking after them while they laboured. The knockers were even known to guide the men in the direction of the precious ore.

By offering my humble donations to the shrine, perhaps I had stirred a few knockers, and they were simply coming to say hello? Maybe I missed my chance at striking it rich? I will never know. But if you ever visit the mine at Real del Monte, take something for the knockers, as now you know, they might be watching.

Exploring some knocking down the Mine, Real del Monte Mexico, 2002

A spooky spectre

Later that same afternoon, we visited the English Pantheon. This cemetery, although neglected in parts, is a striking example of Victorian gothic architecture. Celtic crosses are one of my favourite symbols of Christianity and there is an abundance of them here to admire. There is further evidence of skilled stonework throughout the place. A stone angel looks east towards

England. I also looked east as I treaded quietly throughout this place. There is a certain beauty and tranquillity here. Then again, I picked up on something a bit more sinister. The rain and fog seemed to play their part in getting us to leave too. Bolts of lightning followed by thunder were kicking off in the distance. This grabbed all our attention and we decided to head back to town. Our guide looked relieved as we hopped back on the minibus. He then told us that its best to leave before dark as there have been sightings of the *Dama de Negro* -the Lady in black.

Curious, I asked him to elaborate on this local legend. He explained that when the fog descends over the cemetery it can make the terrain difficult to see and navigate. The townspeople believe it is intentional. People have seen the lady gliding in the air. *'Tourism has never been better'*, he said, *'but I'm not one of those guides that brings people here at night. I respect the spirit and do not wish to encounter her.'* He took a small rosary out of his pocket and kissed it as we continued walking down the hill. Intrigued by the conversation, I spoke to different locals that evening who gave me this detailed description of Real del Monte's very own, *Lady in black*.

Legends says she is an otherworldly figure, a restless spirit who wanders the main road into Real del Monte and through to the cemetery. She is often seen at dawn or dusk, accompanied by a thick fog. She glides silently through the cemetery's iron bars, moving among the headstones as if seeking a specific grave. But whose?

English Cemetery (Panteon Ingles),
Real del Monte, Mexico, 2002

A monument to J.J. Clifford

Perhaps these next stories can shed some light on a local mystery. As we mingled with the local towns people that afternoon, we came across the same story based on two actual events, occurring at the same location. Despite these incidents taking place **a century apart**, they are both connected to an unsettling figure that continues to haunt the road between Pachuca and Real del Monte.

Travelling along this route, you will see a stone marble monument standing in memory of Mr. J.J. Clifford, an American engineer. The exact details of his death are unclear, but speculation paints a grim picture. The official report of 1951 states that he stopped along the road leaving his automatic car running. Whatever the reason, in his haste, he forgot to engage the handbrake, causing the vehicle to roll back onto the narrow road. In a panic, he rushed over, even losing his shoe in the process, but was unable to regain control of the vehicle. Tragically, the car plummeted over the edge, throwing him on the rocks below. The impact killed him instantly, while the car, being heavier, tumbled further down the ravine. All that remained to alert the authorities was a single brown leather shoe on the side of the road. When Clifford did not return home that evening, his worried wife, accompanied by a friend, went out searching for him. The shoe was the first thing they found shortly before discovering his lifeless body on the rock. In the years following his death, a monument was built at that very spot to remember him.

After hearing this, I felt compelled to learn more because the circumstances did not make sense. The road between Pachuca and Real del Monte was one he knew well, a route he travelled regularly for work. Why would he stop in such a precarious spot, especially when safer places were just a little farther down the road? Leaving his car running on that treacherous curve seemed like an odd and uncharacteristic mistake for someone so familiar with the dangers of the area. The unanswered details gnawed at me, so I decided to dig deeper. In my search, I came across a story that sent a shiver down my spine. It seemed that Clifford's accident might not have been the first tragedy here. About a century earlier, another incident had unfolded at the very same spot.

The name Jagos was given to me by a local who still has a family connection to the area and mining community here. He said there was a story about a man named Jagos who disappeared somewhere *en route* between Real del Monte and Pachuca. A wrecked carriage was later seen lodged in the ravine below. When word of the accident reached town, only his wife went out in search for him but it was already too late. People claim to have seen her running through the streets. After that night, she was never seen again. Nothing was ever found and the thick bush and unforgiving wilderness offered no clues. Even stranger, the precious cargo he was transporting was also missing.

Speculation grew. Some whispered that the *knockers* (spirits said to inhabit the mines) might have been involved. While typically helpful, these spirits were also believed to punish greed. Had the man fallen victim to their wrath? Others suggested that Jagos was never in the carriage, having staged the accident to escape with the fortune. The truth remained elusive; a puzzle lost to time.

But perhaps *she* didn't vanish entirely. For years, travellers have reported strange encounters along that same stretch of road. Early in the morning and at sundown, when the light begins to fade and the portal between realities is suspended, a mysterious figure is said to appear. A slender woman, draped in a long black dress and petticoat, her face hidden behind a veil of fine black lace walks along the side of the road. She is la Dama de negro—the Lady in black.

Locals will warn you not to travel alone along this road. Solo drivers seem to have a better chance at meeting her than groups. Some say she raises her hand, signalling for a ride to the English Cemetery.

One chilling encounter comes from a man I met called Don Refugio. He took me to see Clifford's monument and show me where he met the Lady in black. He now refuses to drive alone along this stretch of road and only agreed to take me here because his wife comes down every week to clean the monument on behalf of the local authority. We spoke about his experience while she cleaned the marble stone, coming over to listen in as he got to the juicy bit.

He walked over to the spot and began by saying that he never spoke to her directly.

'She called out to me, telepathically as I came driving past the bend. It startled me, yet I felt compelled to

*stop. As soon as I pulled over, she was already in the
back seat. It was her-the Lady in black.
When we reached the cemetery, I pulled over to let her
out—but she was already standing next to the car. I had
not heard the door open or close. I then caught one last
fading glimpse of her in the distance as the fog engulfed
the entire cemetery, closing it off to the world.'*

'*Me dejo la boca abierta*!' he said, which translates to
being left *jaw wide open*. If you could see his big round
eyes and bewildered stare as he spoke to me, you'd be
compelled to believe him too.

Others in Real del Monte have had encounters with her
on the way past the old church. A pair of tourists claim
to have seen her wandering the town during a full
moon, her figure flickering in and out of the shadows.
She sometimes appears in a busy crowd especially
during nighttime celebrations, or if it's the Day of the
Dead. She is a shadow you catch a glimpse of. Your
intuition senses something *paranormal* is happening.
Blink, and she is approaching. Blink again, and she is
behind you. Turn around, and she is gone.

What is the *Real* truth?
I do not think we will ever know the truth regarding
both tragedies. The connection between Clifford's
death and these spooky encounters remains shrouded
in mystery and leaves a lingering sense of unease that
refuses to be dismissed by locals and tourists alike.
One thing is certain: Cornish or not, if you travel the
road between Real del Monte and Pachuca in the early

morning or at sunset, you may well encounter Mexico's very own, Lady in black!

Crossing the Atlantic

I am happy to report that my friends and I spent our last night in Real del Monte free from any paranormal encounters. We all slept like babies, comforted by the warmth of our shared experience. Still, as I lay in bed, drifting off to sleep, I could not help but think about the people who once journeyed all the way from England to mine in this spectacular location. Did they miss their homeland? What a life! To be born in Camborne and to live, work and die in Real del Monte must have been a daring feat. These brave people lived the meaning of adventure. They paired courage with grit in the hope of finding their fortune in faraway lands.

As for us, we left the following morning under a hot Mexican sun, having enjoyed a breakfast of pasties and bidding farewell to Real del Monte and its legends. At the time, I thought I was leaving it all behind, but life often has a way of planting seeds we do not immediately notice. Two years later, as I began searching for universities to pursue my studies, England kept creeping into my mind. It was not something I had planned or even consciously desired, but the thought of England persisted. Eventually, I decided to apply for a master's degree in psychotherapy and counselling at Regent's College in London. *'Why England*?' my father asked, perplexed. We had been considering NYU and other institutions with familiar names and reputations. Regent's College London seemed random to him.
 '*I don't know, Dad*' I said honestly, '*It's just a feeling*'.

It turned out to be the right choice. In January 2003, I landed in London. Riding the Heathrow Express into Victoria Station, I sat across from a poster advertising a place called St Ives. The image of the turquoise waters and sandy white beaches caught me off guard. Surely this was not in the UK! It looked more like the Caribbean than England. I did not know St Ives was just a few hours away. When you are new to a place, it takes time to ground yourself, especially in a city so diverse and bustling as London. I set the thought aside and started to view that poster as a consistent presence in my daily commutes. It was present everywhere I went—on the tube, at bus stops, in magazines—and each time, the image caught my attention.

I also recognized another poster with a dark figure standing in the background—a lady I once heard about in Mexico. In Real del Monte locals call her *la Dama de negro*. In England she is *The Woman in Black*. In this tale she is more horror than sorrow but still, I find many similarities with our Cornish Mexican *Dama de negro*.

The Woman in Black's author was inspired by classic ghost stories from around Britian. Knowing that our *Dama de negro* is older than the book by at least one hundred years confirms that this story originated in Britain a long time ago. It must have landed in Mexico via the Cornish miners who adapted it to fit perfectly with the environment and hardship of life back then.

Chapter 2
Obsidian dreams

Moving to London in my twenties was an overall fantastic experience. I particularly enjoyed the opportunities to see art and expositions from all over world. I recall one themed around Aztec, Olmec and Mayan cultures. The invite showed a beautiful jaguar mask made of obsidian stone. It immediately captured my attention and reminded me once again of my trip to Real del Monte. Obsidian is a volcanic glass that forms when hot lava cools quickly. Obsidian sculptures and jewellery are still popular today and continue to have huge symbolism rooted in natural mysticism. I purchased several little statues myself while travelling through Mexico, including a little statue of a black panther.

With images of panthers in my mind, my thoughts turned once more to the distant shores of Mexico, where I left that small piece of Cornish history. Even though the Cornish expedition of 1824 to Real del Monte was a lasting migration, some people had to have come back. The surviving records in Mexico held by the descendants of the migration show that 90% of the Cornish population married into the local Mexican population and settled there permanently.

Unwilling to accept that the story ended in Mexico, I felt the need to explore one last crumb of evidence. This tiny nugget of possibility, if true, could hold the key to a two-hundred-year-old mystery that's been terrorizing the British countryside.

Exotic animals and the Empire

Many years before it became illegal to have wild animals as pets, a lad named Willam Cobbet spotted a big black cat on Bodmin Moor. The account was recorded in 1820 and spread like wildfire throughout Britain. This small piece of historical journalism is evidence that exotic animals were being brought over under the British Empire and for whatever reason, some ended up being released into the wild. Many of these animals would not survive due to the nature of the British weather-with one exception and that is Cornwall. The jet stream transports warm air and water from the Caribbean which helps to protect Cornwall from severe frosts and long winters. This is why some tropical and subtropical species survive well here.

Knowing this, we can now continue the story from Real del Monte to a smaller country in central America known then as the British Honduras- or *Belize* as it is better known today. Back in the late 1800s the British were interested in exporting mahogany and logwood from the country, but some exotic animals were also exported to Europe on British merchant ships. These were sponsored by private collectors including Queen Victoria, who was herself a great lover of exotic animals. During her reign, parrots, monkeys, reptiles and many more species were brought over to live in private collections and zoos. There were also many private agents sent by wealthy collectors to retrieve exotic animals and art.

One such agent was Jon Jagos, a Cornishman who left Mexico to pursue work in British Honduras. He was a *jack of all trades* and when convenient a privateer. With him came a short and stalky half Cornish, half Mexican lad of about ten named Jon Jr. They were unrelated other than the fact that the lad's mother was a Cornishwoman from the same town as Jagos. She died of fever in Mexico when the boy was two and never revealed the identity of the boy's father. The boy had straight jet-black hair and chestnut brown skin. The only sign that gave away his Cornish roots were his steel blue eyes and small facial features, identical to his mother's. He was a good-looking boy with wits and courage to match. Skilled in speaking Cornish as well as English, Spanish, and several local native tongues, he worked for Jagos in the domestic sense and as a translator. They earned their keep by hunting and acquiring exotic animals for shipment back to Britain. It was not a warm relationship, but it was built on a mutual understanding that each had something the other lacked.

When Jagos broke the news that he was heading back to England with the precious cargo, Jon Jr. felt a terrible pinch in his stomach as if the world was once again abandoning him. In his despair he blurted out '*I can help you catch a really big cat if you let me come to England with you!*'
Jagos leaned in closer and looked at Jon jr. dead in the eye '*Ya' best be telling me the truth lad* '. He chuckled as the lad's steel blue eyes welled up with tears. Jon Jr. composed himself, tying his jet-black hair into a neat ponytail and reached into his bag to reveal a pouch. Out

of the pouch came a small obsidian mirror. It was so polished you could see your reflection in the smoky glass. *'I got this from Ballam'* he said lifting the mirror up to Jagos' face.

'What is that?' he asked as he reached for the mirror. The boy quickly pulled back his arm and slid the mirror straight into his pocket for safekeeping.

The boy explained that he met a shaman who could guide them to a panther's drinking spot and he had already gone as far as arranging a meeting.

Jon Jr. kept the truth of the experience private. When alone, he'd take out the mirror and stare at it intently. The light reflected a feline figure back at him. This figure appeared in his mind, making him return to the events of that night. As he recalled, he found the shaman sitting by a Mayan temple. He remembered taking a sip of balche (a local hallucinogenic drink used for Mayan rituals) from the shaman's cup. They sat on the ground and prayed to the ancient gods. After some time praying, Jon jr. witnessed a large body of water appearing before them. The jungle receded until there was only water as far as the eye could see. On the other side of the water appeared three leopards, walking side by side. They bowed down to drink from the water. When they lifted their heads, they were in fact, lions. Three lions looking directly at the boy. The shaman chanted and danced as the boy transformed from human to panther.

The image then vanished into the obsidian mirror lying flat on the leafy jungle floor. The moment had past, and minutes had somehow turned into hours. It was now nighttime. The rising noise of a bustling nocturnal jungle was the first sound that woke the boy from his post-trance sleep. With one deep breath, he sat up, looking at the night sky with wide eyes. A line of twinkly stars grabbed his attention showing him the way across the sky and then down to the jungle floor where his is gaze landed on the obsidian mirror. In one quick move, he sprung up, grabbed the mirror and dashed into the night. The shaman, who was lying with his back to all this, remained deathly still, trying his best to quietly conceal his panther eyes and deep incisors under his human hands.

The very next day Jon Jr. convinced Jagos to dig a cage pit next to the temple's waterfall. They left a live pig inside the trap for the panther. Jagos could not believe his eyes when the next morning a panther was indeed, inside the now locked and secured cage. He knew this would fetch the greatest sum of money he had ever seen and could not wait to load the ship and set sail.

A journey fit for a Queen

The journey from British Honduras back to England was a long and difficult one, however the HMS Eliza was especially commissioned for the transport of exotic animals. She was lovingly dubbed 'Eliza's Arc'. None of the sailors were quite prepared for a panther as they brought the cage onboard. Sailors looked on with fascination and fear. Once settled, the creature paced up and down the cage- occasionally growling at those who dared come too close.

The journey back to England in those days went through the Caribbean Sea, docking in Florida, then north along the Carolinas and through to New England for fresh supplies. When they arrived in Bangor, Maine, three months later, they realized that the panther was, in fact, female and heavily pregnant. Her large belly and extremely aggressive growls alluded to the fact that her gestation was soon ending. They decided to stay in Bangor until the animal gave birth. How that panther managed to not only survive the journey to Maine and still give birth to two cubs whilst in captivity, was nothing short of a miracle.

On June 19th, 1881, after stocking up on extra barrels of fresh water, hay and livestock, the HMS Eliza set sail for Bristol harbour. By the time they reached the Cornish coastline, it was clear something had gone terribly wrong. The authorities managed to identify the ship form the remains of the wreckage and a few pages from a personal diary. They detail some odd happenings onboard the ship as they approached the British coastline:

'A sailor came to see me in a terrible state this evening, claiming he had seen not one, but two adult panthers in the cage. On closer inspection, he recognized the boy Jon Jr. sitting next to the creatures. He was caressing one of the cubs on his lap. The sailor then panicked upon seeing the cage door wide open and ran out to come get me.

I insisted he was wrong and went to verify it myself. We found the cage door closed and Jon Jr. standing outside of it holding a small obsidian mirror. Unimpressed by the sailor's clumsy mistake, I asked if he had started drinking salt water again and sent him to rest for the night. The next day I overheard the same sailor speaking to three other men about the encounter. Voices muttered in agreement that a supernatural presence had boarded the ship. Since that day, every man keeps to himself and the crew converse only with their own kind and in their Cornish tongue. The men exclude the captain and first mate from these conversations for fear of being punished for their superstitions'

What really happened may have eluded the authorities but I can tell you that back on the ship, Jagos was unaware of the darken mood plaguing the crews' minds. He was too busy coming up with a way to treble his wages thanks to the birth of two new cubs! As they neared the British coastline, he opened a bottle of rum and toasted to the end of the successful voyage. His relationship with Jon Jr. had become strained on purpose. He wanted to rid himself of the lad once and for all. He invited the captain and the first mate to join him in the galley for a celebration. Jon jr. observed how the men got drunk and played cards. He made himself scarce and when no one was looking, hid in a cupboard.

Neither Jagos nor the captain were aware that the first mate and crew were planning to wreck the ship for personal gain. Instead of heading north into the Irish Sea then onward into the Bristol channel, the boat was sailing west, towards a specific Cornish beach where a band of privateers waited to pick the ship clean.
As the night advanced into early dawn, Jagos let spill to the captain that he intended to sell the boy too as part

of the deal. '*He's not a real Aztec, but he's close enough!*' he laughed out loud. The boy overheard the conversation from within the cupboard and decided then and there Jagos' fate.

As the ship approached a coastline of cliffs and lush inlets, Jon Jr. carefully placed the obsidian mirror on the top deck. He could still see the moon high in the sky as his eyes widened.

Half an hour later, a drunken Jagos came stumbling down into his cabin calling out for Jon Jr.

'*Jon Jr! Jon Jr! Where are you, you insufferable little rat?*' he shouted out.

He sat back onto his bed clumsily pulling off one of his boots. As he looked up, he saw the boy on the other side of the room, sitting under the moonlight. Jagos stood up and took two drunken steps towards the lad. His arms reached out, hands ready to grab the child by the neck. The boy disappeared into the dark leaving the last of the moonlight shining on a King James bible.

Jagos stopped and took two steps back. He looked into the darkness with cautious suspicion. Before he could reach for his knife, a pair of golden eyes and huge white teeth appeared. The female panther lunged at Jagos' neck, breaking it on the spot with one clean crunch. Holding both cubs in his arms, Jon jr. carefully tip toed his way behind the panther and out of the cabin while she devoured her prey. He met another sailor by the side of the ship and placed the cubs in a wooden box. Both Jon Jr. and the precious cargo carefully made their way down the side of the ship landing safely on a smaller rowboat that had been patiently waiting for them this whole time.

Back in America, Jon Jr. had bribed the first mate and six of the sailors into helping him escape when they reached Cornwall. Speaking to the men in Cornish made him Cornish in their eyes. They respected the boy's tenacity and could tell there was something special about him, and so they agreed to deliver him safely to shore-as long as he did not interfere with their plan. From that moment on, the boy knew he'd be safe among his mother's people.

As the sun slowly made its way up the horizon, a dark and deep guttural growl emerged from below deck. Seagulls flew off the ship's mast in a unison cry. Time suddenly seemed to stand still.

From the shadows of the ships' lower deck came a long, black figure. She creeped low and elegantly making her way across the ship's top deck. Three sailors nearby froze as the majestic queen of the jungle made her way past them. The sound of the sea beneath the boat seemed to fade out leaving only the sound of beating hearts. One of the men raised his fingers as if to signal to the others to stay put.

She had their complete attention. Her growls turned into deeper purrs as she reached the edge of the ship. With one graceful jump she leaped overboard and landed in the calm waters below. Her figure glided through the turquoise-blue waters like a wet seal. She swam around the small rowboat once and remained by its side, escorting the boy and her cubs as the sailors rowed towards the docks. The boy looked up at the land in front of him. Seagulls, fishing boats and little white stone cottages lined the inside of an idyllic cove.

Jon Jr.'s eyes caught sight of a flag waving back at him. Three lions on a red background bearing witness to the arrival of the boy and his panthers.

Above: Three Lions of England
Below: The melanistic jaguar or black panther

What hides in the moors and walks in the mist?
While the story I told is fictional, it is true that big cats and other exotic species have roamed the British countryside for the last 200 years. The most common sightings for big cats have been across moors and heathlands. These landscapes are a common feature of the English countryside and Cornwall is no exception. A moor appears as an open plain almost barren and windswept at first due to its altitude, but you soon find plenty of evidence of small shrubs, grasses, bog mosses and damp peaty soils. Prone to mist and fog, people and animals who have gone missing in the moors, have rarely been found alive! Those wishing to hide themselves from the law have often taken their chances with the highwaymen, the spunkies and the beast; but which one of these is real and which is simply folklore?

A very British beast
The Beast of Bodmin Moor is a story that is well known across Cornwall. Sheep and cattle have gone missing or found torn to pieces leading many locals to be weary of travelling through the moor after sunset. The dense and chilling fog that encompasses this landscape can be disorientating, adding another layer of danger.

Today it is illegal to keep certain exotic animals as pets in the UK. This has unfortunately led to some owners releasing their pets without any consideration for the animals' welfare or the general public's. An example of this can be seen at Hampton Court Park, located just on the outskirts of London. It has become home to many exotic birds, including canaries and parrots. These non-indigenous birds either escaped captivity or were released by their previous owners. How these exotic birds survive through the British winter is testaments to mother nature's ability to adapt and survive. The lack of natural predators in the greater London area has also contributed to a rise in their population. Further afield in the home counties, they would be quick and easy prey for the red kites and falcons!

Coming back to the West Country, one exotic pet owner and eccentric, Mary Chipperfields claimed that she let loose three young pumas onto Bodmin Moor when her zoo closed in 1978 while Benjamin Mee, admitted releasing a breeding pair of pumas from Dartmoor Zoo in the 1980s. Is it no wonder these animals have been spotted over sixty times across Bodmin Moor? Newspapers love publishing sightings of these animals and even the local government felt compelled to investigate the matter. The skull of a large cat was found as recently as 2010 along the banks of the river Fowey. Aside from this, they could not confirm or deny the existence of these big cats in Cornwall!

The White Hare

If you manage to elude the beast of Bodmin, you may have to look out for another animal whose presence foretells of misfortune. One such tale written by an author known only as M.H. tells a story associated with this native hare.

This is the story of a naïve young woman named Agnes Garth whose innocence was taken by a man of false virtue named Hubert Arlegh. He was a social climber and had no interest in her other than for his immediate pleasure as he sought to look elsewhere for a rich woman with whom to marry. Agnes was an orphan without a dowry or connections to polite society. All she had was her youth, her beauty and an education. She was hoping to become a governess before she crossed paths with Hubert. He promised her marriage but then demanded that she keep the relationship a secret. When a year passed, Agnes became impatient and went to see Hubert demanding he make good on his promise to her. Hubert already had a fiancée by then, a wealthy Cornish woman who was set to inherit a large piece of land and had a handsome dowry in tow. He cast Agnes aside accusing her of being an easy woman and insulted her further by denying he knew her to anyone who asked him about her.

It is said that Agnes, in her grief at being cruelly castoff by Hubert, went walking into the moors. The dark and the fog may have caused her to become disoriented or maybe she was lured into the peaty bog by mysterious bright flickering lights. However this came to be, she fell in and sank to her death. Was she lured in by the spunkies or did she go down on purpose, hoping to find an end to her suffering and humiliation?
After her disappearance, a search party formed, with Hubert among the men sent to find her. Several people witnessed a white hare following him around. He started to lose patience with the animal and attempted to shoot it, but the hare was too quick for him. He then grew fearful of the animal, knowing full well that its omen was not a good one. Later that afternoon, the excursion to the swamp led the men to discover Agnes' bonnet with strands of blond hair still attached to it. When they dragged the mud further, up came beautiful

Agnes, her cadaver perfectly preserved by the bog. Upon seeing her, Hubert lost his footing on the porous rotting wood planks below and in his fright, fell into the swamp *'uttering a shrill and bitter cry.'* When they managed to drag his body back up, the once handsome and plucky Hubert Arlegh was now cold and dead. The phantom hare had not failed to identify or predict the fate of the culprit!

Magic can be helpful

Not all encounters with animals are as macabre as the tale of the phantom hare. I myself have come across two helpful creatures when I lost my way trying to get to Lizard Point. It is quite common for technology to be rather unreliable in this rough and rugged land, so I was not surprised when my sat-nav froze and turned off in the middle of a country lane. There were no physical signs on the road to direct me and the fork up ahead lacked any signage. I was stuck with three choices in front of me. I asked myself, *'what am I going to do?'* Then, as if by magic, a large hare and seagull came out of nowhere, and onto the road in front of me. The hare jumped up as if to get my attention and the seagull directly above it squawked at me as if to say *'Hey! Look over here!'*. Naturally, I blinked twice as I could not believe what I was witnessing! I hesitated for sure! *'What was going on?'* I thought.

Unsure of what to do I started reversing my car but then the hare jumped out again and came closer, along with the seagull. They both took the path to the left of me and then disappeared. I decided to follow that path and to my surprise, about ten feet down, a signpost for

Lizard Point appeared telling me I was going in the right direction! How could this be? I don't pertain to understand why they decided to help a lost tourist, but I was very grateful. Cornwall's magic never fails to impress me!

Woods that should come with a warning

For my last place of interest, I want to share with you what may just be the ideal location for a spooky encounter! One of the last remaining wonders of the ancient world, *Wistman's wood*, is situated on the slopes of Devon's west Dart river, in Dartmoor national park. This delicate ecosystem is Britain's last remaining temperate rainforest. Here you will find unique species of plants such as the dwarf oak tree, with its stunted growth and contorted branches that hang down and brush the forest floor while others push into the rocks like skeleton fingers wearing a mossy glove. The name '*wist'* is believed to mean eerie, uncanny and pisky-haunted! The entire wood is a treasure-trove for rare mosses and lichens making this an area of outstanding, if not, slightly strange natural beauty. During the day this place is fascinating, but as soon as the sun sets and the fog rolls in, it becomes a very scary place indeed! Here you will find stories of people being led astray by mischievous piskies and spunkies. It is also said that the hounds of hell come out of this wood in search of unbaptized children.

One such tale is of a farmer who went into the woods to hunt. His wife had recently given birth to a baby boy. She was weak and pale. His younger children played in front of the fire while he told his wife his plans. He did not care for the stories of haunted woods. '*It is just old wives' tales!* he said to himself. '*I'll be back in time for supper with a meaty hare*' he told his family and left on foot. It was dusk and he knew he had to make the most of the light. Luckily, it was a full moon too, so he decided to stay a bit longer. He caught the first two rabbits easily, but they were small and not very meaty. Further ahead, he spotted a pair of large pointy ears. He aimed and took his shot hoping to get the rabbit. To his amazement, the bullets did no harm.

When he looked closer, a tiny head popped up and a little man dressed in brown and green looked back! His face was quite ugly, and he had the most exaggerated features: hairy eyebrows that went from ear to ear and a large nose pointing down towards his protruding overbite. He had leathery wrinkled cheeks and tiny beady eyes that seemed to have a permanent squint. The little man yelled out '*Oi! Get ye' home man for there be no hunting in the Devil's woods! Be ye' gone or be ye' dead!*'

With that warning made clear to him, the farmer decided to make his way home. As he walked along the footpath, he heard the sound of hoofs galloping towards him. Before he knew it, the sound was getting faster and closer. The full moon hid behind the clouds making it practically pitch-black. He could not take one step further as he felt his entire body freeze with fear. Out of this darkness, a tall figure dressed in black rode past with three hounds in-tow.

The farmer assuming this was another hunter making his way home, let out a small sigh of relief. He then shouted out '*How did the hunt go?*' The dark figure threw a small but heavy bundle at the man and said, '*take that*', then darted into the trees at Wistman's wood. According to the farmer, the forest opened up taking the rider and his hounds deep into the ground. When the farmer opened the bundle, he found the body of his little baby boy! In his shock and horror, he ran home thinking only of his wife and children. When he opened the door to their little cottage at the edge of the woods, he found her sitting by the fire, breastfeeding the infant. She looked up at her husband and said '*You look like you've seen death m'dear? Whatever is the matter? What have you got there bundled up?*'

At that point he threw down the bundle from his arms and as it fell, a large hare came tumbling down onto the floor. He turned around to look behind him, as the front door was still open, and in the distance, he heard a voice shout out, '*Baptize ye' children or ye' won't be so lucky next time!*' It was unclear whether this being had switched the bundles or if the horseman had played a trick on the man.

The farmer grasped the lesson quickly and without overthinking it. The following Sabbath, they baptized all their children, and he never went hunting in Wistman's wood again! There is much more to discover about this place but on this occasion, I shall leave it you to decide if you are brave enough to venture in.

Above: A white hare
Below: A highwayman/horseman

A mossy stone circle, Wistman's wood, Devon

Chapter 3
The Sacred Waters

As mentioned in earlier chapters, traveling to Cornwall in the past was extremely challenging. When the Cornish mainline railway became operational in the 1850s, it opened the Cornish economy to visitors, marking the beginnings of modern tourism. Even in the 1950s and 60s, Cornwall had no major roads—just winding country lanes and bridleways. In 2024, the new A30 dual carriageway was finally opened to the public, making travel more convenient. These modern developments have not changed the fact that Cornwall remains a land of sea and cliffs, where a wiggly country road will almost always lead you to a breathtaking view of the Atlantic below.

The White Lady and the British Riviera

Before reaching Cornwall, you can stop in Devon. This West Country county is also known for its pristine waters and stunning coastline. It is an ideal option for a short break especially if you are time limited and want to make the most of the West Country without driving deeper into Cornwall. I recommend going to Lydford Gorge, home to a magnificent waterfall known as the *White Lady.* The walk down is steep and slippery so take good shoes. Bring a towel too if you wish to dip your toes!

In Devon we find the British riviera. Starting in Torquay, it extends along Devon's southern coast. As soon as you arrive, you can feel the humidity in the air and the lush surroundings tell you, you are in the West County! My favourite place for a quick break is undoubtably Totnes.

This town is full of independent retailers, coffee shops and a fantastic open market. I love the food in the West Country. It's the best in Britain. West Country milk, butter and cheese are among the best in the world! You will also find all the modern health trends like home-made kombuchas, sauerkrauts and kimchis which are delicious! They have a farmer's market just off the high street that is well worth a visit. I always buy a selection of locally grown mushrooms as well as goat's cheeses. The people are lovely here and I always end up staying for ages catching up with them and getting their first-hand recommendations on where to eat and visit. This town is all about spiritual healing and balance, so you will find plenty of crystal shops, reiki practitioners and yoga classes too.

Totnes High Street, Devon

Here is a little secret between you and me: Walk up St. Peter's quay, turn left onto the Sharpman Estate footpath. This route offers a scenic trail through woodlands, pastures, and fields, providing a picturesque experience. The river below is beautiful too. Along this path you will pass a majestic tree. It is unmissable for its presence and energy. It stands alone overlooking the river below. It is an elemental being because of how it calls out to me. Once while sitting and meditating under this tree, a man who looked like a wizard zoomed by on his bicycle. I opened my eyes sensing his presence. He spoke to me in a warm and happy tone, saying *Ah! You know!* and gave me a big smile as he cycled past. So, you see, in Totnes, I find myself once again amongst my brethren!

An iconic arrival

At this point, it seems fitting that we leave Devon behind and head straight for the Cornish coast. Let us travel to one of Britain's most iconic and historical beaches: Perranporth! This expansive beach extends for miles and is characterized by a unique quality that is both invigorating and uplifting. I still remember the first time I stood there. I had an out of body experience, you can say. From the beach's carpark, I took the long walk out to the edge of the shore passing the different areas of the beach. When I reached the water's edge, I was immediately struck by its unspoilt beauty. It was truly breathtaking! I took a deep breath in, absorbing the beauty form every corner of my vision. The moment made me weak in the knees. A sudden gush of wind then pushed me forward and pulled me up. Before I knew it, I was away on the breeze. I looked down and saw my body standing on the sand. As I went flying on the wind, I travelled across the beach to the top of St Piran's Cross and then back down onto the shore. I passed the caves beneath the cliffs and made my way along the golden sand until I was back in my body again. It was a seamless experience where my consciousness remained a quiet observer of the moment. A tear rolled down my cheek as I went back into my body. I noticed immediately the cold breeze on my arms and legs.

This is the same beach where legend claims St Piran arrived on a boulder. Sentenced to death back in Ireland for preaching his faith in Jesus Christ, Piran was chucked into the sea chained to a boulder. But the boulder did not sink. Instead, he caught a wave and surfed across to Cornwall landing on the beach at Perranporth! St. Piran's flag, a white cross on a black background, represents the white tin he discovered in the black rock. It is also a symbol of the everlasting power of good over evil. So, let this flag be a symbol to all who believe in the power of love! I always wear a small pin of St Piran's flag on my coat to show the world not only my love for Cornwall, but more so my faith and trust in God's plan for us all. God did not abandon Piran, and he has not abandoned us.

St. Pran's Day is celebrated on 5th March every year
Above: St. Piran's cross, Cornwall

More to discover

Cornwall has so many beautiful beaches, there are books entirely dedicated to them! Here are a few of my favourites:

Porthcurno Beach: Voted Cornwall's best beach time-and-time again, why not see what all the fuss is about?

Kyance Cove: It is a tough walk down the steep steps but so worth it when you discover a slice of paradise here on earth!

Bedruthan Steps: When the tide recedes go and explore this magnificent beach. If the tide is high, take in the view by walking along the top. Simply breathtaking!

Mermaids in Kyance Cove, Cornwall

The Bedruthan Steps, Cornwall

A place to connect with nature: St Nectan's Glen

I next want to take you to a unique waterfall, said to be the final resting place of a mythical dragon. The waterfall's cascade has shaped an impressive stone circle out of the rock beneath it. This walk invites you into a realm of undoubtable high spiritual vibration. Mystics believe that the dragon sleeps behind the waterfall at *St Nectan's Glen*. If you stand in front of it, bare foot and ankle deep in these holy waters, you will be blessed.

I had a marvellous experience a few summers ago when I met a traveling cohort of Dutch women on a spiritual pilgrimage. We instantly hit it off as if we'd know each other for years. They invited me to mediate with them in the water and so I did. The sensation of holding hands and chanting together brought me such happiness and is a memory I will always treasure. Before I left the group, the leader came up to me and said, '*I can see your aura and you are beautiful!*' That is the best compliment I've ever had! My encounter with this waterfall opened my eyes to the power of nature and its connection to the human spirit.

A simple church

The walk to St Nectan's glen starts at a little carpark. As you walk up the road you will come across St. Piran's well and a bit further up, his church. I visited the church in early June when the bluebells were in full bloom. An abundant mix of blue, pink and white flowers decorated the pathway leading to the door of the church. The air was rich with the smell of spring.

When I arrived, I was alone and had the place to myself. I sat down in one of the pews and as if by design, a beautiful ray of light came in through the stained-glass windows and warmed the side of my face. I felt such peace and comfort here. It was the ideal moment to pray and give thanks. Cornwall is known as the land of many saints, and it is no wonder why. Such mystical surroundings can only be testimony to Gods' power and grace.

St. Nectan's Waterfall, Cornwall

A Spiritual Place

To get to the waterfall, you must first follow the river. It flows in a poetic way creating a melody with the birdsong that is quite enchanting. As you walk along, you may sense the presence of nature spirits and elemental beings vibrating among the trees, plants, and in the water. Look out for *faerie stacks* too: small mounds of stone built upon each other like a Jenga! These stacks represent wishes, remembrance, thanks, or prayers. If you build one, why not make a wish and you might catch a glimpse of the little people carrying it away to be done! I have recorded orbs and strange lights flitting past with my phone that I only saw after the fact.

This is an excellent place to sit and meditate. I always hum that magic sound: *OM*. This is one of the easiest ways to ground yourself and focus your intention. Take a moment to find a spot that feels right to you. Sit and when you are ready, take a breath in while closing your eyes and say *Ommmmm.* Do this three times and feel the invisible thread connecting you to every living thing around you. Know that you belong here and you are part of the great cosmic family. Nature loves you; the Universe loves you; God loves you. *Om is the word*. You can also hum *Amen* if this feels right. With every breath you take, you are taking in this mystic power. Smile as you do this and know you are welcome here. You are always welcome here.

If you need healing, find a wooden stick as long as possible and walk with it along the river. Find a suitable place to stand firmly and safely. Place one end of the stick in the river water while keeping a firm grip onto the top. I call it *standing like Moses parting the red sea*. Always stand in the direction of the flow and let your rod be the bridge between that thing you are struggling with or still holding onto and the river. Let go of what is holding you back. The river will take it from there. The river teaches us the power of letting go and keeping the waters flowing. The power of letting go gives you the space to receive. That is what the forest around me whispers.

If you do not have a staff or a rod, then simply remove your shoes and stand in the shallowest and safest part of the stream. You can also do this in the ocean. If the water is moving it can create a passage for healing. When we shower, are we not cleansing ourselves of dirt, sweat and grime? And where does this dirt go? Down the drain! In nature, we cleanse ourselves of this modern static and find ourselves at peace.
Further up the river, you can visit St Nectan's cell. You will find ribbons tied to the trees known as *clouties*. Again, these are here in memory of a loved one or to give thanks and prayers. Why not add your own and create a protective invisible thread between you and this magical place?

A Holy well within a beachy cave
Although there are many scared wells and waterfalls throughout the West Country, there is one which is of particular beauty and of spiritual significance. It is the holy well and St Cuthbert's cave near the village of Trevornick. It is out by the northern side of the beach

where most people pass by without knowing it exists. Author John Cardell Oliver's description of it remains as true today as it was then:

This well has Nature only for its architect, no mark of man's hand being seen in this construction; a pink enamelled basin, filled by drippings from the stalactitic roof, forms a picture of which it is difficult to describe the loveliness (Guide to Newquay, 1884)

This well within a cave is where St. Cuthbert's remains were hidden from Viking invaders. Upon reaching the well, his body touched the waters, and they became a powerful source of healing energy. Since then, pilgrims and ordinary folk alike have been coming here to be cured of their pain and illness. You can only access this well in low tide as it will be cut off from the rest of the beach when the tide comes in, so be sure to check! Moving on from waterfalls and wells, we find islands in the sea. Take St Michael's mount, for example, located on the southern coast of Cornwall. It is the smaller counterpart to Normandy's Mont St. Michel. Wait for the tide to be low so you can travel across the causeway by foot! It is truly a memorable experience and well worth the visit.

The mighty Camel and Tamar rivers
When it comes to rivers, Cornwall boasts two magnificent ones: the river Camel and the Tamar. Both are in themselves, powerful elemental beings. They protect and nourish the nature around them, creating a lush and fragrant landscape! I am amazed at the size of plants and trees in Cornwall especially when I compare

them to the same species that grow in my home county of Hampshire. Cornwall has a mild, wet and humid oceanic climate which makes it ideal for plants and animals all year around.

The Tamar river, named after the faerie princess Tamara, began as a bubbling stream and then *she* became the river, running deep through Cornwall and naturally dividing it from Devon. Christian folklore says that the devil dares not cross the Tamar into Cornwall for fear of becoming a filling for pasties! Given that Cornwall is also the land of many saints, there is little hope for him here!

On Cornwall's north coast we have the river Camel rising from Bodmin, reaching estuaries, quarries, and other streams. This is not only an area of outstanding natural beauty, it is also known for birdwatching and something more! Dunbar sands or Doom Bar as it is now known, was cursed by a mermaid. She shallowed the waters on purpose making travel by boat almost impossible. There have been over 600 beachings, shipwrecks and capsizes since records began due to the sand rising. Mermaids or bucca as they were known in the days of old could be helpful beings from time to time but, are hunters of man! Their song could either be enchanting, luring people to their doom or they come at you with a wailing and frightful screech that paralyses you.

Mermaids have been known to feed off sailors, searching for them on shipwrecked vessels. Survivors stranded on the rocks have been dragged down into the depths of the ocean by the bucca. If you do fear them, then stay away from the shallows of the river Camel as this is where they lie in hiding! Take *The Mermaid of Padstow* for example. She was last seen at Hawker's cove brushing her hair on the rock. A young man fell madly in lust for her. When he realized she was not a woman but in fact a mermaid, he shot her in the heart. Before she died, she buried herself under the shallows making Doom Bar the dangerous passage it is known for today.

Another way of putting it is, there are places where humans are not meant to go and Doom Bar sands is one of them. These tales serve as a warning to the curious, the ignorant, and the young. The Buca tell us that the ocean is not to be toyed with or taken for granted. If we cannot stop a wave with our hand, what makes us think we can survive an encounter with the Buca?

I have one last piece of evidence, and it is based on fact, not legend. Cornwall is one of the few places in England where the drinking water is soft. Its low mineral content makes it incredibly light, tasty, and particularly refreshing. Some even say the water in the West Country is pure. It nourishes, refreshes, and protects the mind, body and soul. Travellers report seeing a marked improvement in the condition of their skin and hair whilst in Cornwall. The rock formations make it so, cleaning the water as it passes through. I always bring back a few litres of Cornish water and treat myself to the refreshing taste back home.

The White Lady, Devon

Chapter 4
If not by Sea, then by land

Driving west from southern England or south from Wales can often feel like you are going through a spiritual portal. You notice a shift as soon as you enter the West Country. If this is your first time heading west, then the journey will be your initiation. So, if by land, take note of the first big boulder you see! Try to remember its shape as you make your way through the portal. I am referring of course to the neolithic sites sprinkled all over southwest England. The great advantage of travelling by car is that you can stop at different points along the way.

The Silent stones

My first voyage west took me to Stonehenge, in Wiltshire. This is probably the most famous stone circle in the world, and you are sure to get a good look at it as you drive past on the A303. If you can, do stop and visit this magnificent place! You will also see plenty of little mounts scattered around the site itself. The stone circle itself projects an enigmatic energy that can be picked up with special electro-magnetic gadgets. You will see plenty of people there studying this phenomenon as well as others who view this place as a site of pagan ritual. I was extremely privileged to have been invited on a private tour at sunset. I was able to walk among the stones, touch them and meditate inside the circle. It was amazing and had a profound effect on me.

 If you are coming from further north, you can stop and visit the sacred stones at Avebury Henge. The difference between these two sites is that at Avebury you are free to walk among the stones and feel their calming energy. Until recently, experts believed the stones at Stonehenge came from a quarry in Wales, but new theories suggest they came all the way from Scotland! Were the early Britons compelled to move these stones for a sacred purpose? Or, could it be, that the old Cornish legends about giant's throwing stones for fun may, in fact, hold some truth?

Stonehenge, Wiltshire

Above: Avebury henge, Wiltshire
Below: Men-al-Tol, Cornwall

Evidence of a shared history

These scattered boulders, standing stones or *megaliths*, mark a trail that takes us deep into the Cornish hills, moors and woodlands. Similar stones are also present in northwestern France (Carnac), the Celtic homeland of the Bretons. Both France and Cornwall have a historical connection that dates as far back as the stone age. In Charles Thomas' book, *And Shall These Mute Stones Speak?* he proposes that Cornwall was originally inhabited by Irish Celts to the west and Welsh settlers to the north. He also proposes that Christianity did not reach Cornwall until the year 400AD when further influence from Gaul (north-west France) superimposed Christian-Roman engravings onto ancient stones.

A merging of the old ways with new symbols can be found in the village of Madron where an ancient and holy boulder stands proud. You will see a large cross aged by time. The stone is dedicated to St Madron, a hermit monk who died near Land's End around 545AD. The chapel was constructed over what was already an ancient Celtic holy site. Author Charles Thomas believes that Christianity did not take hold of Cornwall as quickly as we think. The stones and quoits of the old pagan days continued to be of ritualistic use among and unconverted and scattered communities. These places were incredibly treacherous and difficult to reach. A strange mix of pagan and roman symbols remain for us to see. Writings such as *'A' son of 'B'* or just a name and a cross indicate that these stones are for remembrance. Cornwall was the first county in England to make stone crosses even if its conversion to Christianity took much longer. However crudely they appear to us today, these stones are a remarkable and priceless piece of history.

The Madron Cross, Madron, Cornwall

Jack Spriggans and his legacy

If we dive into ancient folklore, the Celtic and Nordic people of Europe all share tales of a time when humans lived in fear of giants. The land of the giants in Norse, Scottish, Norman-French, and Irish mythology was a faraway place that held many dangers for humans. Before we could read or write, we told. Passed down through the generations, all legends and tales adapt according to the times.

Here the Cornish reference to *Jack* is used to denote a lack of identity such as *John Doe*. Jack could be any boy of common descent. He is poor but willing to go on an adventure to improve his life. He is called *Spriggans* to denote his youth and tenacity. The legend of Jack and the beanstalk can be found throughout the West Country and as far south as Britanny, in France. Like David and Goliath, this tale celebrates the bravery of the boy who got rid of the unwanted bully! Nature is also present throughout the tale showing a close connection between magic and the natural world.

The red rocks of Chapel Porth

Travelling to Carn Brea, near the town of Redruth, I find hundreds of stones covering the top of this moor and yet just a short distance away and within an eye's view, the ground around the beacon of St Agnes stands bare. Not a single stone! How is this possible? The legend goes that a giant named Bolster used to terrorize these parts by hunting children. He was known for hurling huge rocks with great ease and would walk in large strides, causing the land to shake. He fell in love with a young woman named Agnes and was determined to keep her for himself. Agnes (or Saint Agnes as she later became known) asked the giant to prove his love for her by filling a small hole in the ground with his blood. Unbeknown to Bolster the hole led straight to the sea at Chapel Porth, and he eventually died having been drained of his blood. The rocks on the beach at Chapel Porth remain red for all to see. Today the St. Agnes Bolster festival celebrates the giant's defeat every May and you can go for yourself to see the proof! I must add that this is also a stunning walk along Cornwall's north coast.

Whatever the origins of these beautiful rocks scattered across the West Country and beyond, we understand that there was an extended period before Christianity where the people lived with a different understanding of their environment. The druids or holy men and women were the keepers of the pagan ways, and they worshiped a more natural life cycle. This does not have to conflict with Christianity or any other religion as I see it. There is nothing wrong with giving thanks to the sun or finding yourself meditating under the moon. You are doing what humans have always done. You are simply acknowledging and celebrating the beauty of the world. So, as you visit these scared places, try and evoke the mystic within you and see if you can feel the awesome presence of the place in which you are. If anything, I find it fascinating to still find the thread between paganism and early Christianity here in Cornwall. Thanks to its distance, difficult terrain, and treacherous seas, these ancient stories and legends have been able to survive just that little bit longer for us to enjoy.

Looking for more evidence of pagan worship, we come across another neolithic site- Men-an-Tol, or the holed stone. Located between Morva and Madron, Men-an-Tol is an impressive megalithic stone that fascinates and bewilders! How is the hole so perfectly round? Legend says that those who crawl through it, are soon cured of their ailment. It is said to be a mood raiser, making those who go through it more joyous and content. Children are particularly drawn to it and you can see them going in and out with glee, So, if the stone calls you, then do not refuse it!

I am told that many of these stones, rocks and boulders are in fact elemental beings and the simple act of sitting on, next to or under them can bring peace and connection. Make sure that you are allowed to first! By knocking three times, you will awaken the stone and you can begin to meditate. Allow your mind to rest and simply notice what is happening around you. You might find the stone speaking to you by means of intuition, visualizations or words that pop into your mind.

More Stone bothering ahead

If you just drove past Stonehenge on the way west but did not stop by, do not worry! You can visit more sites further west! Below are some of my favourites and are a must see if you are in the West Country. I have added the Google reviews of other travellers, so you see it's not just me who finds them fascinating! All these sites also have phenomenal views across the land and make for great country walks!

The Merry Maidens Stone circle-*Atmospheric and beautiful...Went around and touched all the stones for luck!* (Max Colborne)

Boscawen-un Stone circle- *Probably the most peaceful and unique stone circle I have ever visited. A very magical place to recharge your batteries* (BaseTVOriginal)

Duloe Stone circle-*A beautiful and rare quartz stone circle* (Joescad)

King Doniert's stone *-An interlace pattern is carved on three sides of the stone* (Zobo 75)

Carn Euny Ancient village *-Beautiful village with remains of houses built during the stone age* (Nuwan de Zoysa)

Trethevy Quoit *-The best example of a stone age burial chamber in Cornwall* (Eric Bidmead)

Lanyon Quoit *-Just 4 stones, 3 supports and a lid on top of them, but this place is magical* (Nigel Troake)

Druids, dragons and magic

For those who are seeking further connection to those ancient times, then a journey via Glastonbury is a must. It's close to Stonehenge so you can visit both sites in the same day. Glastonbury is more well known for its iconic music festival and new-age vibes, but I'm interested in a hill that was once an island in a marshy sea. The ancient Britons called it Ynys yr Afalon -the island of Avalon.

At the top of this hill, you can see the Glastonbury Tor. The land all around it is believed to also be a giant zodiac. There are streams and underground waterways all over the site, so if you are sensitive to vibrations, you will notice a rumbling under your feet. At the very top of this steep and windy climb stands the Tor. Ancient Britons believed it was a gateway to the land of the dead and so, is known as King Arthur's final resting place.

You can sense the energy as soon as you arrive at the base of the hill. It gets stronger the closer you get to the Tor. At one point I experienced a powerful presence that I can only describe as a rather terrifying and unnatural gust of wind. It seemed to come at me from every direction. I wasn't alone in this and saw several people experience this and turn back!

I was not going to give up and literally prayed my way to the top. Five Lord's prayers exactly. When I finally arrived, I sat back at the base of the Tor, exhausted but grateful. Once there, I basked in its power, taking in the panoramic views from the top.

If you are planning to climb the Tor, be warned as there are no barriers between the path and the side of this hill. Going on a sunny day with good walking shoes is the best way to enjoy this magical and powerful site.

On your way back, I recommend stopping at a second point of pilgrimage: the Chalice Well. This quiet and serene garden with a holy well and stream are known for having ancient healing powers. I always take an empty water bottle and fill up from the lion's fountain. The water here is safe to drink and a few drops in a glass of fresh filtered water is sufficient to enjoy the healing benefits of this sacred site. According to legend, the cup of Christ was brought back from the crusades and buried here. As a result, the well's water has a higher iron content that stains the waterways' border red and leaves a metallic taste.

Glastonbury Tor, Somerset

Standing under the archway, Glastonbury Tor, Somerset

The Holy Chalis Well, Somerset

Statue of Arthur, Tintagel Castle, Cornwall

Doorway to a magnificent view, Tintagel Castle, Cornwall

Walking in the footsteps of King Arthur

In Glastonbury, I cannot help but feel the presence of the *old ways*. Pagan rituals performed on a solstice night remind me that I am standing in King Arthur's land. Back then, England was called Albion, and it was most likely the last Celtic kingdom in western Europe. The legends of King Arthur became popular in the late Middle Ages with *The Canterbury Tales*, 1392 AD; and then again in the age of Romance :1798-1837AD. Today, these stories continue to be popular throughout France, England, Wales, Scotland and Ireland and are testament to our shared history as Celtic and post-Celtic nations. It is now difficult to separate factual figures from fictional ones, and this doesn't matter because in both cases, there is a revival of the old ways which allows us to come back to the source: spiritual mysticism rooted in nature.

Birthplace of a Legend and the link to Wales

Once in Cornwall, you can link your visit to Glastonbury with Tintagel castle! This is the site of king Arthur's birthplace. Ruins of a once proud fortress remain perched on the edge of clifftops with panoramic views throughout. The suspension bridge linking one end of the site to the other is also impressive. Further ahead, you can take the stairway down to the beach and turn left. On a large rock you will find a face engraved in it. It is Merlin and his cave is a stone's throw away. I always feel a mystic presence here.

If you are a fan of these legends, then you must make a note to travel a little further north, to Wales. It came as no surprise to me to learn that once upon a time, Cornwall and Devon were also known as southern Wales. Evidence of a round table can be found at Caerleon castle deep in the Welsh countryside. Other sites in England and France dispute this but, I have it on good authority that Wales is Arthur's homeland. As king of the Britons, his territory extended from Wales into southern England, including Cornwall to the west and possibly as far south as Brittany in France. His surname Pendragon also has Welsh roots. The Welsh flag itself is represented by a red dragon standing proud on top of a white and green background. Although this flag was made famous by the Tudors, the legend of the dragon goes back at least a millennium. Every Welshman knowns that dragons are born green (like all reptiles) and upon reaching adulthood, turn red.

Looking back at Merlin's face edged on the rock I decide to find out what became of him. According to legend, Merlin left Camelot with the fairy Vivienne and hid in the forests of Brittany. Afraid of being abandoned by the wizard, she trapped him in a stone prison deep in the forest of Broceliande. If you go there and follow the trail, you will see what remains of Merlin's tomb: two large megaliths leaning in on each other, symbolising the power of attraction. You can visit this place and see for yourself if this is what became of them. Could they have become elemental beings? Knock on the stones three times and see if you sense their awakening.

The gardens of Cornwall, a natural connection

What is England if not a garden? The West Country is no exception to this saying. In Cornwall, the grand estates and private gardens are just that little bit *grander*. As I mentioned in previous chapters, nature here grows on another level. An abundance of rich nutrients in the air and soil allow for plants to grow and flower all year long.

Connecting with the natural mystic involves simply being present in it while allowing your intuition to guide you. Look at the plants and in your mind's eye, speak to them. Use your inner voice or your outer voice, if you don't mind people thinking you're away with the fairies. Compliment the nature around you. Don't be afraid to touch or hug a tree. You can gently caress the plants you come across with your hand or find a spot that calls to you and sit there for a while. Breathe in and as you do, know you are inhaling the healing air of the gardens around you. Nature is the cure. So go and restore yourself with the plants, the trees and the sounds of birdsong.

I mentioned in earlier chapters how the plants in Cornwall are on another level! So be prepared to see some huge ones! And yes, these sites all have gift shops should you wish to take a bit of Cornwall home with you!

Trebah Gardens. As mentioned earlier, is home to the US Navy. Here you will find stunning gardens with trails to discover and get lost in! You will need a whole day to discover this magnificent place.

The Lost Gardens of Heligan. Another site with beautiful grounds to discover and connect with nature. This is an ideal location for families and small children. Take a picnic and spend the day enjoying the biodiversity found within these grounds.

The Eden Project. A wonderful selection of different biospheres. It doesn't matter if it's raining outside because most of it is indoors! You'll need several hours to truly enjoy this place. You can take your own lunch, but the project hosts a variety of food stalls with dishes from around the world.

Lanhydrock House and Garden: Dubbed Cornwall's most beautiful estate. It boasts a large manor house with impressive architecture and the grounds are a mix of landscaped gardens, a riverwalk through woodlands and their own holy well! Plenty of routes for bike riders too.

Lanhydrock House and Church, Bodmin, Cornwall

Chapter 5
Knockers at the Great Flat Lode

I feel I have now come full circle with you, gentle reader as we arrive back in the mines! This time, we are no longer in faraway lands, but back home, in Cornwall. Discoveries in mining techniques and engineering allowed Cornwall to be the first county to enter the industrial revolution. Towns like Redruth and Camborne were created to house the communities of minors that thrived here for over a hundred years. The mine at the Great Flad lode is perhaps one of the finest examples of industrial mineral extraction. It lies under the granite slopes at Carn Brea in an unusual shallow way. A 'lode' refers to the mineral vein itself. Copper and tin were extracted here until the site closed in 1920.

A walk around the grounds makes for a worthwhile outing. You can visit many of the buildings and areas used for mining ore. The land around the mine is now grassy and pleasant. A peace has returned here, and it is welcomed and needed. The towns of Camborne and Redruth today are an example of a poverty and isolation that is so typical of Cornwall's history. A stroll down Camborne high street won't bring back memories of Real del Monte. I am met by a parade of boarded up buildings spread among the charity, off-licence and betting shops. People with toothless grins and squint eyes toasting to better days, greet each other warmly on opposite sides of the street. The homeless here, as tan as leather chairs and smelling of alcohol, congregate on the small square while a quiet and meagre market takes place. I wonder if there are any families left that could still be linked to the original expedition? *'Perhaps it is I who have returned',* whispered a spirit in my ear. *'From Real del Monte to Camborne, a journey now complete.'*

As I heard this, an old man waves at me through a shop window and says *Cheerio!* I realize I have been staring into space and am surprised to see his reflection in the window instead of mine. He laughs out loud, as do the people in the shop. Embarrassed, I make my way back to the car.

The Cornish Giant

Moving on with my day I come across some defunct train tacks now sleeping in green pastures. This brings to mind a long forgotten Cornishman named Richard Trevithick. His genius created the first steam engine train. In 1804, the locomotive transported seventy men with ten tons of iron over a nine-mile track. He continued to design steam powered road vehicles, ships and most importantly, pumps for mines. This improved working conditions by allowing water to be pumped out instead of carried out manually. *Another* great invention by Trevithick.

Origin of the knockers

I have been asked many times if I believe in the myth of the knockers as being the souls of the Jews who killed Christ and were sent here as punishment to work in the mines. In simple terms no. Despite my efforts, it has been impossible to trace the original story because it does not exist. There is no physical evidence of any Jewish settlers or merchants coming to Cornwall nor are there any written records in religious or historical documents. This is a good example of just how far antisemitism spread throughout Europe, arriving very late into Cornish myth. The link between Jews and gold is also another widespread misconception. We know that early Christians were not allowed to lend money, but the Jewish bankers and merchants could, often acting as brokers. Finally, the fact that when the Cornish arrived in America in the mid 1800's, this detail was dropped in favour a more natural and mystic understanding of the caves proves there was never any truth in this.

The lost caves

One last possibility linking the origin of the knockers to the mines could be found in the fogous (pronounced foo-goo), naturally formed underground tunnels only found in the most westerly part of Cornwall. There are fogous in Ireland and in France as well, but here in Cornwall, there are at least 15 known locations. *Halliggye fogou* near Lizard Point is a fine example of one. These passages date from the iron age. Roman coins amongst other artefacts have been found, making us wonder just how many people have used these tunnels? Historians theorize that these passages could have been used for safety, ritual or storage purposes by early Britons and Roman Britons alike. Could knocking have been a way of communication between people who did not want to be found? Like an early morse-code? We know that the Romans led a strong campaign against the druids in western England around 61AD but they left little evidence of domination in Cornwall. Boudicca, queen of the Iceni tribe is evidence that the people of Briton did not lay down the red carpet for the

Romans. In fact, the roman campaign of Britain was a real thorn in the side of the empire. In Cornwall we find two potential forts near Bodmin and Camborne, but these limited remains are no help in putting this mystery together. Although the Romans were eager miners themselves, they would have had their work cut out for them in this difficult terrain, far, far away from Rome.

What did the Romans ever do for us?

For starters, they gave the Cornish their name! The Romans called Cornwall Cornubia, after seeing how the people decorated their helmets and homes with horns. I often think of the iconic comic book *Asterix the Gaul,* as a good example of a once proud Celtic nation. My final thought on the knockers is as simple as knocking is a good way to find out if the chamber or wall next door is sealed or hollow! Don't we all tend to knock on walls when we're renovating? But what do you do when the walls knock back at you? Do you tell yourself it's just an echo, someone pulling a prank or is there some other force at play deep within the ground? Visitors often describe these caves and passages as mystical, eerie and supernatural.

A walk though Truro

If you are ready for a break from the underground world, then travel down to Cornwall's capital city, Truro. Visit the outdoor and indoor markets for some local specialities then follow the Truro river to Skinner's Brewery. I must admit I always come here for their fine ale and food, and it is always such a pleasure to be among my Cornish brethren! With over twenty different beers named in tribute to Cornish mining such as the *Cornish knocker*, there's sure to be one for you. Another tribute to the miners that still exists throughout Cornwall is the traditional Cornish pasty, although found in Devon too, the origin is the same. This tasty D- shaped meat pie pastry allowed the miners to enjoy a hot meal without running the risk of getting arsenic poisoning. Arsenic was a constant presence and threat to the miners and so they dug it out and sold it as a type of pesticide. When it came to eating underground, miners held onto the outer tougher crust of the pasty so they didn't have to worry about ingesting anything toxic. This savoury meal allowed them to carry on working underground. Perhaps this is where the origin of leaving a bit of food for the knockers comes from: the castaway crusts of the pasty! Nowadays people all over Cornwall claim to make the best pasty and I keep a close watch on this. What else is Facebook for if you can't join groups like *Rate my pasty?*

Side street walk up to the cathedral, Truro, Cornwall

Truro Cathedral, Truro, Cornwall

A healing stream, Cornwall

An elemental being, Hampshire

Part Two

Chapter 6
Into the natural mystic
We now come to the second part of the book where I share with you some of the knowledge passed down to me from the natural mystic. This is an essential chapter for those who wish to know it better. Most people have an immature understanding of spiritual matters. I have come to accept my encounters with nature spirits, elemental beings, angels and ghosts as part of my evolving human experience.

So, I invite you to open your awareness to the presence of all living beings, energies and vibrations. As the proverb suggests: *Enter the forest and observe; the trees are not lost* The presence of a higher power is evident in all things. It is not solely humans who can communicate with the divine; this capacity extends to all creations. Both flora and fauna, as well as natural landscapes, emit a sacred resonance that may be perceived unconsciously, even if modern awareness has grown inattentive to it. Our ancestors practiced a spirituality deeply rooted in this. They acknowledged the mystic power within every being and could interpret signs and messages from nature.

These mystic energies are only found in nature. They are alive and abundant throughout the world, but we place little value on the life of a *faerie tree* or *a healing stream*. As a rule of thumb, we are not meant to interfere with any mystic being but, if you do meet one, then it is meant to be. They do not reveal themselves to those who seek them by force and they are very clever at eluding technology like photography and film.

Mystic Cornwall past and present
In Cornish culture, nature spirits and elemental beings existed here long before man's presence. Every generation sees and defines them in their own way and I am grateful that so much has been preserved about them in Cornwall.

Elemental beings such as trees, mountains, waterfalls, rivers, and rocks are sacred natural landmarks emit a deep spiritual vibration because of their location on earth. These are specific vibration can be felt, heard and in some cases seen. Many consider these elementals as a type of earth -deity. Examples of these around the world are Uluru (or Ayers rock), in Australia; the Ganges river in India and mount Machapuchare in Nepal. They are all holy landmarks and humans understand what is allowed and what is not. I would never disrespect these beings by walking over them, polluting them, or taking a piece back as a souvenir. Remember to leave these places as you found them: with love and respect. Furthermore, it is of the highest importance that we help elemental beings survive. We must do what we can to clean and tidy their dwellings. I often go on littler picks in the forest and on the beach. We cannot access their grace and wisdom if we kill off their environment. Too many people fail to realize the importance of preserving the natural world. This delicate eco-system is far more complex than we ever imagined.

Spirit of the Forest in front of me, Cornwall

Above: A deer among the ferns, Dartmoor, Devon
Below: Pheasant on a fence, Wiltshire

From my travels to Mexico, I learnt that the knockers and hobgoblins are earth spirits that dwell deep in caves, rocks and mines and monitor the earth from underground. Their counterparts above ground are the faeries, elves, derricks, spriggans and piskies or pixies. They can be of air or fire depending on the location. Brownies are a type of faerie that dwell in homes.

Legend says that faeries gave men the gift of music and so it is no wonder they are often described as joyous little beings playing their little flutes and banjos! These beings love it when humans tend to nature. They love watching us garden or tidy up a landscape riddled with rubbish. They bring good luck to those who care for nature, after all it is like someone coming to help you clean and organise your home!

Night lights over a grassy bog
Flickering lights over moors and bogs that lure weary and lost travellers away from the path is the work of the *spunkies*, a type of mischievous fire faerie. In Islam, the djinn are similar spiritual entities associated with a smokeless fire. They can use their powers for good or tomfoolery depending on who they are helping. Like the derricks in the forest, the spunkies and the *djinn* can alter our sense of orientation and cause deja-vu. You'll know you have encountered one if you find yourself lost or stuck and you keep coming back to the same point, over and over. This has happened to me while camping on the moors. It is very frustrating! A wood-witch's advice to me was to find a long stick. Make sure it is bare of leaf and bug. Run if up and down the side of your body. Continue your journey and keep the stick in

our hand. Holding the stick maintains your focus while you walk and looking at it will act as a reminder for you to stay on track.

The other more mystical use to walking with a stick/wand/branch is that all nature spirits recognize a bare wooden stick. It is the symbol of separation and boundary. When we walk with it, we are communicating our intentions of friendship but within limits.

Hampshire Faerie hiding in my garden (stone statue)

What lurks in the sea?

The Cornish coast is home to a wide variety of sea creatures. Whales, orcas, dolphins, manatees, and sharks all visit these waters. The bucca, also known as sea- folk or mermaids live in these waters too. There have been sightings of these creatures by adults and children. They take advantage of the gravitational pull of the moon to come up to the surface and swim closer to shore. If you are fishing at night, you may catch a glimpse of their fishtails; glowing and mimicking the brightness of the moon. They sometimes spy on us in the shallows, frightening children who look down at the water's edge, seeking their own reflection but find a mermaid's wide black eyes and pointy teeth grinning back at them!

Typically seen on top of large rocks or on small sand-islets close to shore, they will move quick and be out of sight before you get a chance to look closer. When they do come into our waters, they hide among the thick seaweed. They prefer to move at night like the octopi and other nocturnal sea creatures. The bolder ones will venture into caves when the tide comes in and hunt for bird eggs and chicks. They will climb up the cave walls, dragging their tale along the rock and collect these delicacies before the tide goes out again. Like ravens and magpies, they like to collect shiny objects such as large seashells, pearls and natural crystals. During the day, they cannot see well so you might catch one if you wear all black, cover yourself in seaweed and put a large pair of sunglasses that cover your eyes and brows. This makes you appear more sea creature than human to them. If you sit and stay still, you may just catch one moving. This is how some locals have come into contact with them and survived.

On the whole, these are wild and mysterious creatures; more shark than human. Cornish folk tales describe them as six foot from head to tail, with long hair that covers their arms and back like a blanket. Their tales are greenish-blue and they have very large eyes.

The Cornish are not fond of them and will tell you it is not good to encounter them.

Many authors have written about these beings from the deep. In fact, psirens and mermaid-like creatures seem as old as time. The Testament of Solomon, an ancient Hebrew book on magic and daemonology names one of these creatures as Abyzou, perhaps taken from the Greek word abyss. These creatures have many names and exist in many cultures. They are a mix of serpent or fish, some with snakes on their head, like the medusa of ancient Greece. What is certain is that these stories have been around for as long as there have been oceans. It is no wonder that centuries later, they found their way to the West Country.

Many stories, one truth

Fact or fiction, what is certain is that the ocean that covers our planet is the oldest of the elemental beings after Mother Earth herself! Scientists believe that water came from outer space, arriving on our planet as a frozen element.

Moving away from water, we find rock and dirt. The earth, its soil and energy gives life to nature spirits everywhere. They decide for themselves where they want to live. There are clues humans can recognize but to do so requires belief, intuition and experience. They do reward the faithful so be patient!

One final word on the theme of piskies and faeries. I have been asked numerous times if I believe in *changelings*, otherwise defined as a being who is half faerie, half human or all faerie but *passing* as human.

There is enough evidence to show that in the old days when a child was born with a disability, weakness, or difference, people would say it was *a changeling* or a *faerie child* that was swapped for a healthy human baby. As a result, these children were abandoned, abused or murdered. This is why I disagree with this notion. Children are a blessing especially for the mystic who is herself, mother to all.

So, to be clear: there is no breeding between humans and nature spirits. Why? It is like trying to mate a bird with a cloud, it makes no sense! Just like computers and mobile phones are man-made creations, nature spirits and elemental beings are Mother nature's creation. They are the unseen workers like the worms in the ground that toil and cleanse the soil. When a deer dies on the road, I have often seen the fog roll in and with it, the faeries coming to carry the animal's spirit back to Mother earth.

Mermaid/Bucca are a mysterious force

Chapter 7 Paranormal encounters

One cannot write about Cornwall and leave out the paranormal. It's many popular ghost stories like the *Screaming skull* and haunted sites like the famous *Jamaica Inn* continue to attract tourists today.

When it comes to their place within the natural mystic, these energies are tense and irritating. Animals, amulets and hair can often pick up the vibration of a haunted spot. These energies left life in an unhappy and unresolved way. They are quite literally kicking and fighting their way into the light, creating a *push-pull* effect that impacts the flow of energy around them. But rest assured, humans are protected by our own life force and its place in the natural order around us. Only God can breathe life into existence. Mother nature is *his lady* and this pact in unbreakable. It is called the Great Mystic Union.

Prisons and asylums are good examples in the sense that their purpose is to hold and restrict the freedom of those who reside there. If you want to experience a haunted sensation that is still very much alive in Cornwall, go to the town of Bodmin. It has an especially important and historic prison called Bodmin Gaol (jail). Impressively well preserved, it is well worth a visit. You can even stay in the Bodmin Jail Hotel, which is part the original jail.

Make sure you book your place as the only way to visit is with a tour. The tour guides have an interest in the paranormal while the tour itself has immersive special effects that bring you face to face with life in prison.

While visiting this place, you will learn the stories of those who passed through its gates: the men, women and children thrown together in dark, cramped and wholly unsuitable cells. Some went to jail for murder, others for stealing a loaf of bread. Ten minutes in those dark, damp and the cold conditions seemed punishment enough of my sins so I was happy to leave as soon as the tour ended. At Bodmin Gaol, hanging was the usual form of execution, but we know there are many ways to die in prison. Many untold stories continue to haunt the prison even today.

While on the tour, we went deep into the jail where one cell in particular made me cry. It was allocated specifically for women and children. I was overwhelmed with sadness by this dark and unsettling space and had a little cry then and there. The heavy energy that surrounds you is a reminder of the sorrow and despair that seeped into every wall of the jail.

Sightings of strange beings are commonplace here. Narrow corridors and dark staircases block the light and fresh air from reaching us *on purpose*. Objects have been known to move around, even hitting tourists, evidence of the strong and enduring disruption to the flow of energy.

I remind myself that these ghosts tell a *human story*. The part about pain and hardship through the ages. We must honour them by seeking out the truth. They say lighting candles can work as the symbol of light in darkness is a powerful one and may help these energies move on. In Christianity, the candle's light is the light of God, and he welcomes all beings into his loving presence.

Bodmin Jail, Cornwall

Above: View from a cell, Bodmin Gaol (Jail)
Below: The Staircase in Scotland

A haunting in the Highlands

As mentioned earlier, Bodmin Gaol is a good place if you are searching for a haunted location. I feel compelled to share with you another similar experience because it does show the effects of a haunting but also, the power of biology, the mind and an imagination that is open to suggestion.

This experience happened about six years ago when my family and I rented an old house in Scotland that I believe was haunted. The house was well over a hundred years old and had gothic vibes throughout. From the moment I got there, a musty smell of old wood, stone and dust caught my attention. I knew instantly. This is a hard feeling to shake. My stay was mostly uneventful, except for a feeling of being watched, especially at night. I think it is natural to find yourself influenced by the environment rather than logic. The paranormal is sensed before it is thought of. Logic comes after the initial scare, doesn't it? We rescue ourselves by saying it is old floorboards or rats in the basement. Most of the time, it is, but sometimes, it is not!

To add another layer of fear (and inconvenience), the only working toilet in the whole house was on the first floor and I was staying on the ground floor. I had to climb the long winding staircase that stood at the centre of the house every time I needed the loo. The thought of having to use the toilet in the middle of the night worried me every time it popped into my head. At night, the large bay windows at the top of the staircase allowed the light of the moon to shine down onto grey painted walls and an oversized chandelier hung from the ceiling. It didn't work properly, so I never turned it on. Instead, I used the torch light on my phone to see my way through.

On the very first night, I left my room to use the loo just after midnight. As I took my first step onto the staircase, I swore I heard the giggles of small children. Then and there, something tripped me! I stepped back and tried again. I tripped, again. I could not avoid tripping on that first step!

Getting back to my room each night required another bout of courage I could barely muster. Well, one night as I cautiously made my descent down the staircase, a heavy goods vehicle drove by, shining its light through the window and onto the chandelier making it sparkle and move vigorously. I then felt a chill run up my spine. *That's it!* I thought, *I am not sticking around*! I ran down the stairs in a panic and jumped into bed next to my husband. I hid myself under the duvet, holding onto his body for dear life. Petrified, I couldn't get back to sleep for ages and spent the next two hours waiting for the sun to rise. I heard every creek, footstep and other movements throughout a house that should otherwise be quiet.

In the morning, I awoke and told myself it had all been down to an overactive imagination. I shrugged it off and carried on with the holiday. Every night, however, the same thing would happen, and every morning I'd say it hadn't!

The day before we were set to return home, I discovered I was pregnant. Looking at the test tube, alone in the upstairs bathroom, I felt the presence of something looming over me. *'Can I get some privacy please'* I said out loud jokingly, and to my shock, the bathroom door slowly swung open revealing the landing opposite the stairs. No one was there yet I felt a presence. This was unsettling to say the least.

I kept my pregnancy and experiences private but sensed something was wrong. That evening, I did not go upstairs but instead, had a nightmare. In it, I awoke alone in my bed with the long windy staircase in front of me. I then saw that first step and as I looked up, the chandelier was emitting lots of twinkly lights. They reflect onto the walls and stairs like a disco ball.

Then that dreaded feeling of something not being quite right landed in my gut. *Other beings* started coming out from each of the crystals in the chandelier. They landed on the stairs and as soon as they took full form, began fighting each other for a place in my womb. I felt smothered by their presence all around me and awoke, gasping for air and covered in sweat. That's when I noticed even my thighs were wet. I understood then that I'd had a miscarriage.

Was the house really inhabited by spirits or was I in a vulnerable emotional and physical state due to the pregnancy? It can be difficult to separate the paranormal from the power of projection.
On the drive back to England, my husband and children began talking quite casually about our stay in the old

house. The children spoke of a presence they felt on the ground floor landing directly opposite my room, just where the staircase began. I hadn't shared anything with them about my own experience because at the time, I didn't want to upset or worry my family with this, but it goes to show that we all perceived something separately and without influence. My husband joked that it's not Scotland without a few ghosts! We won't be staying there again! But if you're curious about this place and would like to visit, then drop me a line!

The practicalities of hauntings

Regarding hauntings, I do want to mention that traditionally, hauntings were a rather effective and inexpensive way to keep people out if your affairs. The rich and the worried share this in common. It's a genuine possibility that servants, family members, visitors or opportunistic criminals might be tempted to rob an abandoned property. If I were an elderly lady living on my own in a grand old property, I might be tempted to tell a tale of horror just to keep people out! The pharaohs of ancient Egypt knew this and so became experts at warning grave robbers of the mummy's curse and indeed, many books and documentaries have been written on the subject. Just look up the curse of Tutankhamun, among many others!

Of course, today, ghost hunting is a type of dark tourism that relies heavily on the participant's imagination along with enough encouragement on the part of the tour guides. If there is some good to be found in these experiences it is that it brings tourism back to places that may otherwise be lost in time, but I don't particularly like or enjoy this type of entertainment because on the whole, it devalues the memory of the victims.

A love lost in time

My final ghost story is inspired by love and the vacuum it leaves behind in one's memory and heart. Is it possible that a love lost in life can somehow be waiting for you *somewhere* in time?

They say true love creates an invisible thread that is so strong, it can pull people back together, bending the laws of time and space.

This is the information that was given to me by someone from the great beyond. The location is a grand hotel that stands majestically above the ruins of an old castle. People often pay over the odds for the best room but, for me it's the room at the top of east wing of the tower that revealed a story unlike any I've ever experienced.

In that room there is a small black and white picture of a beautiful woman and two children, framed on the hallway wall. Most people enter the room and walk past it without even seeing the picture. It's easy to miss but maybe this is *on purpose*.

The woman in the picture is seen standing at the centre of the photo, holding hands with two small blonde children. They are standing next to the hotel's main fireplace and a large Christmas tree is directly behind them. I believe the photo was taken around the first world war by the way in which they were dressed. In those days, the hotel was family owned and run. She may have been the children's governess or nanny by the uniform she was wearing.

Her kind eyes complimented her warm smile. The children can be seen looking up at her with great affection. Their faces express the sweetest little smiles which caught my attention because as far as I can remember, in most pictures from the old days people usually looked serious and sombre. But this picture made me feel happy. But why keep such a lovely picture on a dark wall? I carried on with my visit and left the room thinking nothing more of the image.

That evening as I was getting ready for bed, a faint twinkle coming from the entrance hall of my room caught my attention. As I went to investigate, I saw a dim light coming from the picture on the wall. The closer I got, the brighter and clearer I could see the little figures moving inside it. Time was rewinding within the picture. I felt compelled to touch it to make sure it was really happening. To my surprise the frame came off the wall easily and fell on the floor. When I picked it up, the light was gone and the whole scene went back to the original picture.

I hung it back on the wall, bewildered by my experience. Then, as soon as I turned my back to the picture, I felt a presence behind me. I stopped and froze for a moment, noticing the gentle pressure of a hand on my shoulder, each fingertip landing in turn on my collarbone. I couldn't believe it and instinctively turned around only to be met with what I can only describe as a *flashback*.

I found myself walking through *her past*. It was the same hotel but it was not as it looks today. It was in the style of the 1920's and a man about 30 years old passes me by. I noticed that he walks with a limp. I am told he was wounded in the Great War and now works as manager in this grand old establishment.

Fast forward to a few weeks before Christmas and the hotel is busy making space for the festivities. Our lady can be seen walking through the reception and stops this man to ask for his assistance. They lock eyes and instantly, a connection is formed. She tells him there's an old lady in a wheelchair in need of assistance. He kindly obliges and goes to help. They both accompany the elderly woman to her room. Before they leave, the elderly lady asks if they are newlyweds staying at the hotel. They both blush and he clarifies that he is the manager should she require anything else.

As they walk back to the main reception, he says she never answered the old lady and then asks if *she* is a guest here, to which she says no. She is the new nanny. He introduces himself as James and she is Berenice.

Over the next three weeks they find themselves drawn to one another over music and poetry but they must keep their feelings secret. Other employees notice them looking at each other just long enough to deduct that they have fallen for one another.

Soon he steals a kiss from under the mistletoe and a week later, he gifts her a necklace. A simple golden chain with a small heart. They spend the next three days walking along the shore below holding hands or sitting by the fireplace in the early evenings after she has put the children to bed.

At the winter ball hosted by the hotel, everyone is merry and our couple is no exception. James takes a picture of Berenice with the children looking up at her. They can't seem to take their eyes off their beautiful nanny and James is no exception. He makes Berenice blush with his constant loving gaze. He has not felt this way since he was a boy. He has not known such happiness and peace since before the war. Despite his wounded leg, he is agile and swift.

But all is not well. James has a secret he must tell Berenice and that is that he is married with a wife in the Cotswolds. On new year's day, Berenice opens the door of the hotel reception to welcome a woman in from the snow only to discover that she is here to see James. Berenice collects herself and disguises her surprise. James is clearly shocked to see Claire but composes himself all the same and quickly falls into the role of dutiful husband. He dares not look at Berenice in the eyes. Employees are quietly talking about this encounter behind doors and in backway corridors.

Door Knocker

Berenice feels humiliated and embarrassed. She is now nowhere to be seen and skilfully avoids him throughout the week, tending only to the children she is governing. He wants to tell her that he is in a loveless marriage. It was done on an impulse before going to war. When he returned Claire had sold most of his belongings to pay for her gambling debts. He came to Cornwall to escape and be forgotten. With a cold animosity, she makes him return with her at once. You see, she's gambled the house and now all may be lost. The following morning, James leaves the hotel with Claire without say goodbye. Berenice wakes to an engine sound in the distance, realizing it is too late.

Winter soon gives way to spring and James finds himself longing for Berenice's kind eyes and beautiful spirit. The months have not diminished his feelings for her and he misses her beyond belief. In fact, he can think of nothing else but her. So, on a cold March morning, he meets with his lawyer and signs the divorce papers making him a free man once again. He can now return to Cornwall and ask Berenice to marry him.

He returns to the hotel on a rainy and foggy night. Two employees greet him with great warmth and confirming him he's been expected. Something is not quite right with the place but it is late, dark and he has travelled for two days to get here. He retires for the night in a staff room, behind the reception area, on the ground floor. *Curious* he thinks to himself, *this accommodation wasn't here before*. He settles down anyway and thinks about Berenice. But really, he cannot wait, so he jumps out of bed and runs to the top floor of the northeast wing to find a dim light coming from Berenice's room. He knocks and when the door opens, a single delicate hand extends out from the room, inviting him in.

The next day he awakes to find he is alone in bed and in *his* room. Furthermore, it is half past twelve in the afternoon and he is due to meet Mr. Enys, the hotel owner at one. He wonders how he got there but quickly dismisses the thoughts and focuses on getting dressed as quickly as he can. He is hoping to get his job back and also, announce his intentions to marry Berenice as soon as possible. On his way out, he recognizes Berenice's gold chain on the floor by his bed. He wonders how it got there and feels a pressing need to return it to her. Instead of going to his meeting, he turns around and makes his way to the northeast wing. As he approaches, he slows his pace then comes to a full stop. He sees that the door to the wing has been boarded up and is hiding behind a makeshift curtain. A workman's ladder stands in front it and a small handwritten sign stands on the ladder's middle step saying, *Northeast wing currently out of use for repair. DO NOT ENTER.*

James is confused. He was in the tower just a few hours earlier. He runs outside to look at the hotel from the courtyard only to see with his own eyes that the whole wing and tower have been destroyed by fire. Every window is blackened and a boarded up. The owner comes outside to find James starring up at the tower in disbelief, his hands covering his mouth. He gently asks James to come inside.

Pouring James a drink, he reminds him its been two years since the fire and money has been tight. He tries to explain that repairs take time and getting the right people for the job has been difficult. *'Two years?'* he interrupts. He has not been away for two years! Mr. Enys shows him the date on the newspaper and James suddenly realizes that it has in fact, been two years since he left the hotel.

He carries on explaining that exactly two years ago, a fire broke out in the kitchen and rose up through the vents of the tower. Mr. Enys remembered seeing Berenice running down the stairs with one child in her arm and the other led by the hand. Once the children were safely on the ground floor, she disappeared into the tower.

Although they managed to put the fire out quickly, they were too late to help Berenice. She was found in bed, and it was clear that she never left her room. The smog created by the flames, took her in her slumber. Mr. Enys believes that even in death, her love for his children compelled her save them. He confesses to James that he found it difficult to explain what he saw. The children seem to have no memory of the event either. James left that afternoon keeping the previous night's experience to himself. Was her spirit perhaps waiting for him to return? More importantly, is her spirit still tied to this place now?

As for me, I felt compelled to ask the hotel about the tower's history. I shall now leave with you with one last eerie detail I found out that morning: The night of my visit was the 1st of March 2022. According to the owner of the hotel, this is exactly **one hundred years to the day** that the northeast wing of the tower burned down.

Pengersick Castle, Cornwall

The Camelot Castle Hotel, Tintagel, Cornwall

Chapter 8
The challenges of faith

The ability to see and interact with the mystic comes when you cultivate your own spirituality. A barrier to this is often caused by our own religious trauma and disappointment. If we were failed by our childhood faith, then the concept of tree spirits could potentially be another crazy idea. The same can be said for atheists. They refuse to see the value in belief and they have their reasons too which should not be mocked or dismissed. All over the world, people have turned away from religion. Just this Christmas, my family and I attended a beautiful Christingle service at our village church. For a village consisting of a couple of hundred people, only a handful of us came to the service. This is a good representation of the state of our churches in these modern times.

So, to those who struggle to move from religion to spirituality, I say go and make peace with your childhood religion and move forward into the next phase of your spirituality. It is time to return to the garden. Those who understand this will be content with all they have.

I understand this takes time. It took me many years to come back. So now, I am learning to be patient with the world, the way God is patient with me. Even when we closed the door to him, He always left a window open for us to return. For me, the window was nature itself. As a mystic and a Christian, it has taken me many years to accept that my love for nature and my faith in God are in fact the same thing: One love. This love brings peace. So let us love the trees, the animals and all the wonders that lie thereof. Nature is where you find evidence of his grace and glory.

Self-portrait, Hogmoor Inclosure, Hampshire

Help from above

We now come onto the topic of angels. These cosmic beings watch from a higher dimension and interact with humans all the time. They protect and guide us towards love and acceptance. We fail to see them as angels when they take human form because they mingle with such ease and fluidity that our suspicions of them being something more than human are always fleeting and quickly forgotten. When they've finished helping us, they simply go on their way without asking for anything in return. They are known to be gentle and patient energies often turning up as a helpful stranger. My aunt in Canada, a practicing Christian, has assured me that angels are real, adding that they are not see-through nor ghost-like. In fact, their human form is just like ours: real to the touch. They bring a calm and reassuring presence to any situation. I do believe there have been times in my life when an angel has come to be with me. I have had many conversations with strangers and not always under stress or unhappiness, sometimes just as a spontaneous chat. Again, these experiences felt natural, real and were not in any way scary. I encourage you to reflect on those random conversations you've had with a stranger. Think back to a time when someone helped and didn't ask for anything in return. How did their kindness and support make you feel? Perhaps we can all open our minds and hearts to the people and causes around us. This divine quality exists in all of us. We all have the ability to be an angel to someone at some point, because this is how the Holy Spirit works.

My friend Ryan, a young man aged about 25 often travels down to Cornwall to go camping and kayak fishing. The spot he goes to is so secret, only a handful of people know of its exact location. The landowner lets him stay for free as long as he tidies up the grounds while he's there. So, Ryan will often spend about two weeks looking after the land in exchange for fishing, kayaking and enjoying his time in nature. It's a lovely way to switch off from his computer-based office job! Anyway, on one particular occasion, he was packing up his belongings and having some great difficulty in getting his kayak back on the roof of his car. No matter what he tried, it kept falling to the point where Ryan was worried the roof rack was broken and he may have to leave his kayak behind.

As he put it, *'Out of nowhere appeared an old Cornish fisherman, his accent so thick I could barely make out what he was saying! The old man picked up the kayak, placed it firmly onto the roof rack, showed me how to make a knot so the kayak would not budge and just as soon as the whole thing was set, he walked off into the nearby hedge and disappeared*. Ryan never saw him again but wondered *who was this man*? Ryan decided to keep this encounter to himself as many of us do. He's been back to Cornwall and to that idyllic fishing spot many times since but has not encountered the helpful stranger.

I suppose we mustn't worry ourselves with the thought of meeting angels because they don't require our awareness of them to be here but they do seem to appear at specific times. Many people have reported the 'third man' factor: a phenomena where a person is in grave danger and they sense the sudden presence of a being that is encouraging, guiding and protecting them during the ordeal. People caught in avalanches or stuck during a natural disaster have been guided to safety while under extreme distress. Afterwards they claim it was a supernatural force that saved them.

The gentle path towards spiritual alignment

Humans are capable of communication with all beings and it helps if we can establish a peaceful relationship with them first. We need to be present, centring our intention towards them and opening our mind and heart to their presence.

Believe it nor not, most nature spirits and elemental beings are also here to help! They too want to see us in our true nature. Nothing gives the earth spirits greater pleasure than feeling the rumbles and stomps of humans dancing, laughing, singing and celebrating life! When you feel ill or insecure, go take off your shoes and walk on the grass. Forest bathing is a lovely way to gently relax and mediate. Especially if you need some space from others or would like to have a time out, simply take a blanket you can sit on and go for a forest walk. Stop and sit when the first tree calls out to you. It will happen in your mind's-eye. Have a seat and just look around you. The trees here are not lost. They know exactly where they are. Stay here and meditate for a while.

If you feel the call, go and hug a tree. Sit amongst them and allow their energy to help you. Stomp around, dance, make positive vibrations. This is the language of nature. Did you know the earth itself is an elemental being? Our beautiful planet, goddess of the solar system is unique and irreplaceable. She has many names: Eden, Gaia and she is our gift from God. She is the valley and he is the valley spirit.

The Holy Light
There is one final elemental being whose existence is of such phenomenal importance, it unites people of science and faith alike. It's light, warmth and energy inspired humans to come out of the caves and into the light. From there, our relationship with nature evolved. The fresh air and light were the first things we noticed when we left the damp, dark and humid environment of the caves behind us.

The light is a powerful ally. Every morning, as the sun rises a pink light emerges. This early light is of such benefit to us that just 10 minutes a day is enough to raise our serotonin levels and create vitamin D! Regular morning walks and spending time in nature has been proven to be more effective or equal to taking antidepressants.
In your own home, the sun can be a great ally in everyday health. Drying clothing in the sunlight kills off bacteria, viruses and fungus and helps to brighten clothing too. Growing your own food and gardening have all been scientifically proven to help you lose weight, improve mental functioning and mood. Letting the sunlight in every morning is also a wonderful way to bring in positivity and joy into your life.

The autumn and winter represent a time when humans must harness their inner light and celebrate a return to life by honouring Mother Earth and God for the gift of life. As we go into darkness, many people around the world kick off the season around late October and early November by celebrating Diwali, the festival of lights. This is a joyous festival for Hindus, Sikhs, Jains and some Buddhists around the world. Then we come to the winter solstice which happens around December 21st. Many pagans gather at Stonehenge and other holy sites to celebrate the return of the light. As a Christian I also celebrate the return of the Son, our Lord Jesus Christ, Light of the world on December 25th. Chanukah is the miracle of light given to the Jewish people in a time of great darkness and persecution. God's miracle saved them and the light of the Chanuka candles symbolise his protection and love for his people, and indeed all who are struggling. The message is clear and the same: light will always conquer darkness.

So, do not let the darkest day define you, but hold on to the light. We all have a candle within us and it is our compass, our talisman and our reminder to shine our light into the world.

Winter solstice over Stonehenge, Wiltshire

Chapter 9
Tuning into a different frequency

In order to congregate among nature spirits and elemental beings you have to be in nature and learn to appreciate and cultivate it. To love nature is to love *them*. Although immortal, without nature, these beings cease to exist. They do no die off easily though. A rose growing through a concrete slab has enough soil beneath it to push through because the earth is an elemental being! Such is the miracle of life. The rose asks not for permission, but opportunity. Seeing a concrete rose will inspire you to dig up the concrete and create a rose garden.

If you wish to congregate among these spirits then go into the forest. Find a row of trees lined with moss and look out for faerie doors: natural openings in the trunk, at the base of a tree. These should be deep and obvious. A feeling will guide you as well. These can also be marked by mossy stumps. Usually, faeries live in cities much like we do so where there is one faerie tree, there are probably ten. These trees often have spikey bushes growing on the tree itself or what looks like a very large and messy birds' nest with sharp twiggy branches poking out from the bark. That's their way of saying stay out! Sometimes people add a little wooden door as an offering which is very sweet and pleasing to these nature spirits but honestly, not necessary.
As a rule, do not disturb them or remove anything. Every bit of moss, every plant and every branch is part of them. Tread carefully if you're going in for a closer look. You can leave an offering of berries, honey, flowers on the floor or on a wooden plate or bowl.

I have often come across the much sought after faerie portal especially in the summer months when the sun sets late in the evening. This is the best time to find one. I have a spot on my walk in Hampshire where I know of one. As the sun sets, the trees and shrubs come together to form an archway. From a certain angle, you will see the rays of light shining through and a different landscape emerges through the portal. It's absolutely beautiful, illuminated with gold and I feel tempted to go through it but I dare not, for fear of not returning! Many such arches exist all over the world but in Cornwall I find them much more commonplace. Unlandscaped areas are the best but sometimes they form despite our desire to tame nature. Many roads in the UK are lined with hedgerows and the trees and bushes can often grow inwards creating beautiful portals that are worth noticing. Some of the most ancient roads dating back to the iron age can be found across southern England and the West Country. These sunken lanes or 'holloways', are gems to travel along and although they do not lead anywhere but the road ahead, they do make you appreciate the beauty of nature.

An encounter with a Hampshire faerie
On my woodland walks I have come across little faeries sitting on the top of trees. In Hampshire, the ones I see most are little brown beings with white cone hats. They sit at the very top of trees and you can easily miss them by mistaking them for twiggy branches. Ah but this is not so!

I met one little faerie in my own garden one summer evening. It was around 9p.m. and I had just finished watering the plants when a cranefly shot out of the bushes and right into me. To my surprise it was an actual faerie with wings! His little brown boots caught my attention as he hovered in front of me trying to gain his sense of direction. He was just as shocked to see me as I was to see him! I clearly saw his little body: half insect, half humanoid. He darted off into the horizon like a sparkler!

While walking in the woods behind my house, I often come across *faerie row*. Bluebells decorate the path along this avenue alerting me to the presence of nature spirits. We are aware of each other's presence here. They are territorial beings so I do not disturb them any more than I have to. I take pictures and compliment them on their beautiful homes. Faeries despise unnatural boundaries such as metal or wooden fences, barbed wire etc. And in my patch of the woods, I see they've torn it down. Maybe the recent storms had more to do with this than faerie magic, but could it be a mere coincidence that this metal wire fence is up all along my walk except for faerie row? They tell me *'No! We need to roam above ground as freely as the roots of these old trees roam underground'*. I see two young deer directly opposite me. They also need to roam free and refuse to be caged in by fences.

Above: Napping on a tree over a stream, Hampshire
Below: Faerie doors, Hampshire

A portal appears, Holybourne, Hampshire

Above: Faerie Row behind my house, Hampshire
Below: Faerie ring made of mushrooms pops up, Hampshire

Faeries hiding in the bluebells, Hampshire

An example of nature-minding

Since having had my own spiritual awaking, I continue to study and research the benefits of spending time in nature.

In every forest you will find some type of elemental being. Trees are the most obvious to spot. Holes and dents that look like eyes are a good starting point. Just this afternoon, for example, I went on a walk in the forest behind my house and straight away I felt the presence of nature spirits and elemental beings. I cleared my mind and focused gently on the moment. I took in the beauty around me: the trees, the fields, the wind and suddenly, I spot a red kite perching on the branch of a large tree further up in the field. I stop and in my mind's eye I ask: *are there any faeries here?* The red kite gives out an unmistakable hawk-like cry and I take that as a *yes*. Up the road, I see the faeries have left a wand for me to take on my walk. '*That's funny*', I tell my husband, '*I was thinking about a wand as we left the house and now a wand is hanging in a bush for me to take*'.

I thanked the faeries and carry this wand with me throughout my walk. As I carefully make my way through a narrow passage in the forest, I see pheasants and a fleeting glimpse of a deer hoofing it deeper into the woodland, evidence that this forest is very much alive! I continue walking and am happy with my wand. I parade it proudly showing everyone in the forest that I am a believer. The trees in this this forest know me by now. I've walked among them hundreds of times over the last six years. I tell them how beautiful they are because it's true! I see their majestic branches, some straight, others curved and then there are the eyes in the bark that I sense are looking back at me. I don't mind, it's nice to be seen just like they must appreciate my admiration for them. Sometimes I go too far and hug and kiss the trees if it feels right!

There is a bit of this walk where I always zip my pockets up or turn them inside out. This is because some of these trees along this naturally formed avenue are inhabited by piskies and they can be particularly mischievous. When the bluebells come out in May and June, the piskies become territorial and we must not go into their patch. Stingy nettles and brambles circle the bluebells. These mark an invisible border between us and them. The same can be said for certain moors and heathlands.

The fallen autumn leaves now cover the trees' roots as I make my way home. The trail is uneven and slippery but my wand is my protection. My time here is always healing and beautiful.

Although this forest is in Hampshire, I am aware of its magic thanks to my time spent in Cornwall. Before visiting Cornwall, I loved nature walks, days by the beach and hiking in the mountains. Now I truly appreciate just how precious these environments are. It is not just the rainforest that needs saving. Our gardens, our parks and our streets all need saving. It is not enough to go and enjoy them, we must also preserve, re-forest and put as much nature back into our lives as we can. As mentioned before, if you want to see these beings, then you have to create the right environment for them. This is one of the things Cornwall has taught me. You do not have to go all the way to Cornwall to feel spiritually connected. This planet is the supreme elemental being. Evidence of the Divine is everywhere. Our planet is not just a gift but a constant reminder of His power and grace.

Nature and spirituality are our allies through life's challenges. If we do not develop a spirituality rooted in peace, then *something else* will take its place. So, let us now mine for a better spirituality, as *peacekeepers* of God's earth. When we look after our world, we become better at looking after each other. This is and always will be the route back to God. Until we meet Again, gentle reader, please remember *Onan hag Oll* as the Cornish say, we are **One and All.**

*Self portrait
waving St Piran's flag,
Truro, Cornwall*

Above: My son, 4, playing on the beach, St. Ives, Cornwall
Below: My daughter, 12, Perranporth, Cornwall

Above: Nature-minding our way down to the river
barefoot with my nephew 3, and sister in law, Hampshire
Below: Love and the Sea, Falmouth, Cornwall

Stone Lion, Pengersick Castle, Cornwall

List of recommended reading on the West Country:

Mullis, D., (2010), *West Country Faerie, How and where to see Nature Spirits,* 2nd Edition, Bossiney Books

Passey, J., (2021), *Cornish Horrors, Tales from Land's End*, The British Library

James, R.M., (2022), *The Folklore of Cornwall, The Oral tradition of a Celtic Nation*, 2018, University of Exeter Press

Caine, M., Gorton, A., (2005*), Walking through Cornish Folklore, Fables, fantasies, Myths and Mysteries*, A Comfy Jack Book

Chorlton, A., (2019), *Cornish Folk Tales of Place, traditional stories from north and east Cornwall,* Mazed

On Nature:

Pogacnik, M, M, M., (2009), *Nature Spirits & Elemental Beings, Working with the intelligence in Nature*, 2nd Edition, Findhorn Press

Wohlleben, P., (2018), *The secret Network of Nature*, Penguin Roundhouse Publishing

On Spirituality:

Myss, C., (1997), *Anatomy of the Spirit*, Bantam Books

Pradervand, P., (2009), *The Gentle Art of Blessing*, Atria Paperback and Beyond Words

Wall, G., (2012), *Deepening the life of the Spirit*, Quaker Books

Bourgeault, C., (2004*), Centering Prayer and inner Awakening*, Cowley Publications

Mabry, JR., (2017), *Starting Spiritual Direction*, Apocryphal Press

Bibliography

Barber, R. (1979), *The Arthurian Legends*, Dorset Press

Corrales, L., (2020), *Sucedio en la carretera a Real del Monte*, El Sol de Hidalgo Newspaper
https://www.elsoldehidalgo.com.mx/analisis/sucedio-en-la-carretera-a-real-del-monte-5902742.html

Institute of Cornish Studies, University of Exeter, Knockers, *Tommyknockers and the Question of Ghosts*,(2024),
https://www.exeter.ac.uk/research/centres/ics/research/thecornishoverseas/knockerstommyknockersandthequestionofghosts/

Mullis, D., (2010), *West Country Faerie, How and where to see Nature Spirits*,2nd Edition, Bossiney Books

Caine, M., Gorton, A., (2005*), Walking through Cornish Folklore, Fables, fantasies, Myths and Mysteries*, A Comfy Jack Book

Pogacnik, M., (2009), *Nature Spirits & Elemental Beings, Working with the intelligence in Nature,* 2nd Edition, Findhorn Press
https://wildernessengland.com/blog/cornish-history/#cornish-folklore

Merlin's Tomb, https://tourisme-broceliande.bzh/en/lieu/merlins-tomb/

History of Dartmoor National Park -Wistman's Woods
https://www.haunted-britain.com/wistman's_wood.htm

Thomas, C., (1994), *And Shall these Mute Stones Speak?* University of Wales Press

Passey, J., (2021), *Cornish Horrors, Tales from Land's End*, The British Library

Oliver, J.C (1884) *Guide to Newquay and neighbourhood, including Perran, Bedruthan Steps etc*. Palala Press

Tabbush, Anna, (2025) *Blow, Blow, Westerly Wind* – shared with permission from the author.
Link: www.annatabbush.com

Printed in Dunstable, United Kingdom